SO-ATQ-968

QUILTS
from my garden

20 PROJECTS WITH RECIPES FRESH FROM THE GARDEN

Have fun
quilting at
Sandra's Stitches.
Karen
Snyder

Karen Snyder

©2008 Karen Snyder

Published by

kp krause publications

An Imprint of F+W Publications

700 East State Street • Iola, WI 54990-0001
715-445-2214 • 888-457-2873
www.krausebooks.com

Our toll-free number to place an order or obtain
a free catalog is (800) 258-0929.

All rights reserved. No portion of this publication may be reproduced or transmitted in any form or by any means, electronic or mechanical, including photocopy, recording, or any information storage and retrieval system, without permission in writing from the publisher, except by a reviewer who may quote brief passages in a critical article or review to be printed in a magazine or newspaper, or electronically transmitted on radio, television, or the Internet.

The following registered trademark terms and companies appear in this publication:
Easy Scallop Tool, JT 606, Hamilton Beach, Ruffino Riserva Ducale,
Singer, Heat and Bond Ultra, Steam-A-Seam.

Library of Congress Control Number: 2007940514
ISBN-13: 978-0-89689-580-5
ISBN-10: 0-89689-580-7

Designed by Katrina Newby
Edited by Andy Belmas
Printed in China

Dedication

This book is dedicated to everyone who enjoys a stroll in the garden and takes the time to enjoy the beauty therein.

Acknowledgments

I would like to thank the many wonderful people in my life who make my work a joy:

My girl gang for their support— Monica Solorio-Snow, Connie Nason and Cortné Stricker.

Melinda Crowley and Janet King for their piecing skills.

My editor, Andy Belmas, for his hard work and encouragement.

Sarah and Judy Hillman for the photography.

Katie Newby for the beautiful design and layout of this book

My family, for believing in me.

The many friends and strangers who opened their garden gates: Jo Fitzsimmons, Melinda Crowley, Patty Jacobson, Robert and Molly Lane, Sid and Bette Snyder, and Peter and Wanda Pawluskiewicz.

This book was photographed on the Long Beach Peninsula in the southwest corner of Washington. Our small beach communities of Long Beach and Seaview have been popular summer tourist destinations for over 100 years. Many of the cottages here have wonderful gardens and gates that are a joy to behold, if we remember to take the time to look. If you can't visit in person, you can visit at www. funbeach.com.

CONTENTS

Gardens come in all shapes and sizes. Whether they are neatly manicured, allowed to run amok, or presented to us as designed by Mother Nature, they bring joy to the onlooker.

In the seaside town where I live, there are all manner of gardens. I can entertain myself for an hour or two just riding my bike up and down the quiet streets, looking at all kinds of gardens. The flowers, shrubs, and trees make a pretty picture, and the garden structures add to the beauty of the scene. Trellises, windmills, old watering cans, and birdhouses add to the charm as well. My favorites, however, are the garden gates. They come in so many styles and shapes.

The gates never seem like they're intended to keep people out, but to invite them in— into a wonderful, half-hidden treasure of a garden. Gates always allow you a glimpse inside. And sometimes—through their slatted fronts or spilling over their support posts or peeking out from the adjoining fence— you'll see nasturtiums run amok, scarlet runner beans doing their best to run away, or whimsical garden art to draw your attention. There's always the promise of a respite when you spy a chair or tea table nestled among the vegetation. And inspiration lives there, too. Inspiration to create quilts and stitcheries that will keep the garden alive all year long.

So please, open my garden gate and come inside. You're most welcome!

THE FLOWER GARDEN

Flower gardens are the loveliest gardens of all. Their only purpose is to please the soul. From the first spring bloom to the last bit of color in the fall, the flower garden refreshes us, reminds us to pause a moment and take in the wonder of nature. Let flowers inspire your fabric choices for the Garden Flower Quilt. Keep your sewing space neat with the Flower Pincushion and Scrap Catcher, and tomorrow morning enjoy a fresh scone with the easy, no fail Cream Scone recipe.

Garden Flower Quilt

Pieced and quilted by the author | Quilt: 79" x 79" | Block size: 14" x 14"

Pretty floral fabrics combine to make a cheerful garden quilt. While this is a large quilt, the pieces that make it are large, too. Combine those large pieces with easy strip-piecing methods and you'll be surprised how quickly this quilt comes together. Use it to bring the flowers indoors or spread it on the grass for a picnic near the garden.

Fabric Requirements

3¾ yd. purple floral for blocks and border
2⅛ yd. yellow floral for blocks
⅛ yd. yellow for flower centers
1⅓ yd. purple for flower centers, inner border, and binding
2⅓ yd. green for setting triangles
4⅔ yd. backing fabric

Cutting Instructions

1. From the purple floral, cut:
   8 strips 8½" x 40" for the border
   2 strips 10½" x 40"
   4 strips 6½" x 40"
   2 strips 2½" x 40"
2. From the yellow floral, cut:
   6 strips 6½" x 40". Set four aside. From remaining two strips,
      cut 8 squares 6½" x 6½"
   4 strips 4½" x 40"
   4 strips 2½" x 40"
3. From the yellow, cut:
   1 strip 2½" x 40". Crosscut into 13 squares 2½" x 2½"
4. From the purple, cut:
   9 strips 2¼" x 40" for binding
   9 strips 2" x 40". Set aside 7 strips for inner border. From remaining two strips
      cut 48 squares 2" x 2"
5. From the green fabric, cut:
   2 strips 13". Crosscut into 6 squares 13" x 13"
Cut four squares in half twice diagonally for side setting-triangles.
Trim remaining two squares to 11". Cut each square in half once diagonally for corner triangles.

Piecing the Blocks

Note: *For ease of construction, you will piece four strata for the blocks. These will then be crosscut and reassembled into the blocks.*

1. For strata A: Join two 6½" purple floral strips and one 2½" yellow floral strip together.

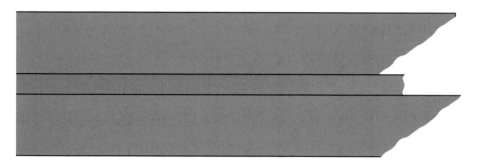

2. For strata B: Join one 10½" purple floral strip and two 2½" yellow floral strips together. Repeat to make a second strata.

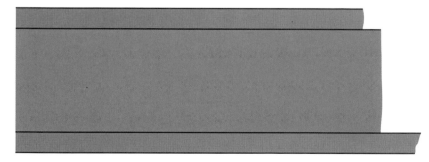

3. For strata C: Join one 6½" purple floral strip and two 4½" yellow floral strips together. Repeat to make a second strata.

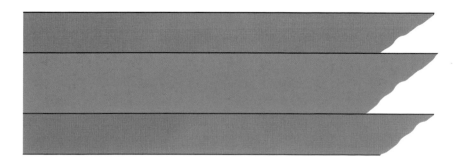

4. For strata D: Join one 2½" purple floral strip and two 6½" yellow floral strips together. Repeat to make a second strata.

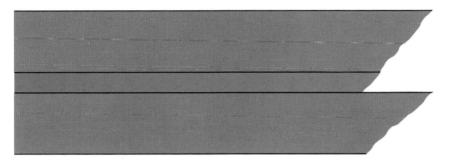

5. Press all strips toward the purple.

Crosscutting

6. Crosscut each of the strata into thirteen 2½" segments.

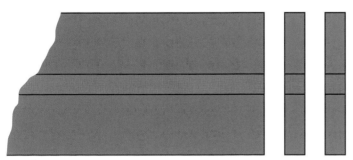

Crosscutting strata.

Piecing the Flower Blocks

7. Arrange seven strips cut from the strata as shown.

8. Join strips together. Repeat to make thirteen blocks.

9. Press toward the center strip.

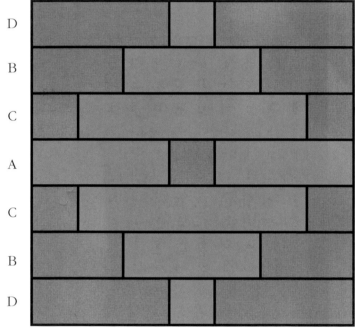

Joining the strata into blocks.

Note: *To make the centers of the yellow flowers, purple corners need to be added to some of the blocks.*

10. Draw a diagonal line on the wrong side of the 2" purple squares.

11. Place a purple square on one corner of a block. Stitch on the drawn line. Trim, leaving a ¼" seam allowance. Press purple square over to replace the corner that was cut away.

12. Add the number of corners in the chart below:

Number of Blocks	Number of Corners
3	2
4	3
5	4

Adding purple corners to the blocks.

Side Setting Triangles

13. Join a 6½" floral square to one side of a side-setting triangle.

14. Add a second side-setting triangle. Repeat to make eight.

15. Add a 2" purple square to each side-setting triangle as you did in Step 11.

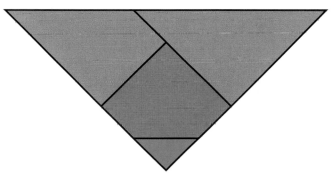

Pieced side-setting triangles.

Assembling the Top

1. Lay out the blocks, side-setting triangles, and corner triangles as shown.

2. Join the blocks together into rows.

3. Press the seams in each row in opposite directions. This will allow the seams in each row to nest with the seams in the row below it.

4. Join the rows together. Press.

Adding the Borders

1. Join all the purple strips together for the inner border by sewing diagonal seams. Press.

2. Measure the length of your quilt lengthwise through the middle. This will prevent you from having wavy borders. Mathematically this number would be 60½", but everyone's seam allowances vary, so be sure to measure.

3. Cut two strips the length of your quilt.

4. Attach one to each side of the quilt. Press toward the border.

5. Now measure your quilt crosswise through the middle. This measurement should be approximately 63½", but check your measurement to be sure.

6. Cut two strips this length.

7. Add them to the top and bottom of your quilt. Press toward the border.

8. Repeat steps 1–7 with the 8½" strips of purple floral for the outside border. Press.

Preparing the Backing

1. Cut the backing fabric into two equal pieces.

2. Remove the selvage and stitch the two pieces together along the longest sides.

Finishing Your Quilt

1. Prepare your quilt sandwich following the Layering and Basting instructions on page 121.

2. An allover design works well on a blended quilt like this. For a little extra pizzazz, you could quilt a flower in each of the side-setting triangles.

3. Bind and label following the instructions on page 122.

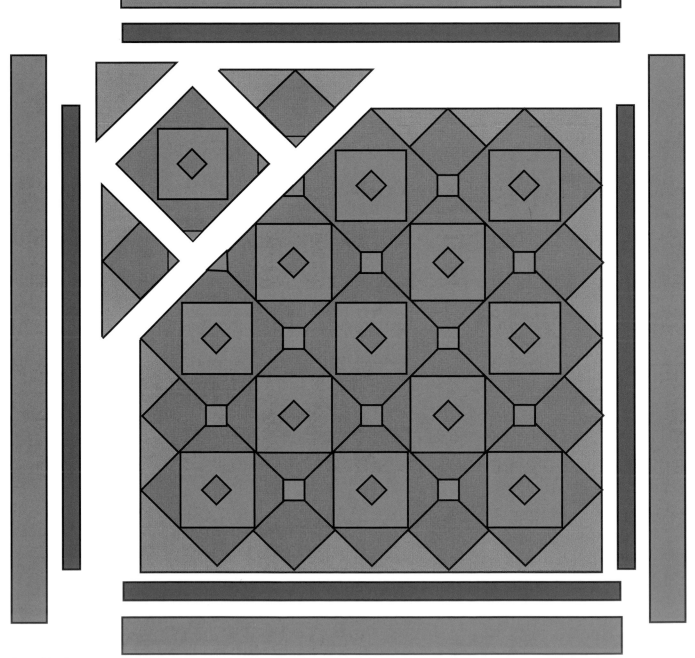

Assembly diagram.

Pincushion and Scrap Catcher

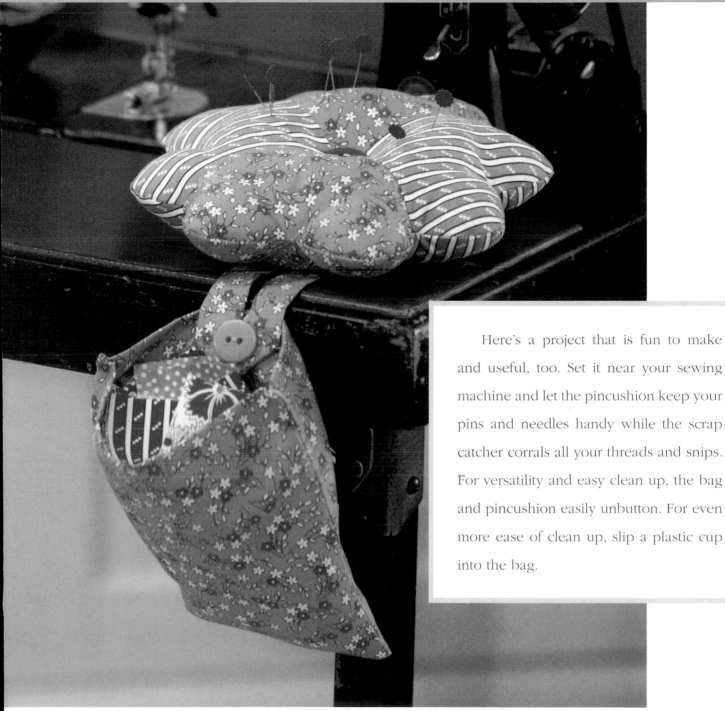

Here's a project that is fun to make and useful, too. Set it near your sewing machine and let the pincushion keep your pins and needles handy while the scrap catcher corrals all your threads and snips. For versatility and easy clean up, the bag and pincushion easily unbutton. For even more ease of clean up, slip a plastic cup into the bag.

Your sewing area will be tidy and your pins handy when you keep a scrap catcher nearby.

Materials

¼ yd. stripe
⅓ yd. floral print
1 cup flax seed
Fiberfill
3 buttons (¾")

Cutting Instructions

From the striped fabric, cut:
    4 squares 4½" x 4½"
From the print fabric, cut:
    4 squares 4½" x 4½"
    2 rectangles 7" x 14"
    1 strip 2" x 18"

Piecing the Pincushion

1. With the 4½" squares, make two four-patch blocks.

2. Place the two four-patch blocks right sides together. Baste around all sides.

3. Trace around Template A in all four sections of a four-patch block. You only need to trace on one of the four-patch blocks.

4. With a short stitch and a ¼", machine sew the two four-patch blocks together following the traced line. Trim, leaving an ⅛" seam allowance.

5. Open a section of seam near the center of the four-patch. This will be used for turning and stuffing the pincushion.

6. Gently turn the petals right side out through the hole.

7. Pour the flax seed in through the opening. This will give your pincushion enough weight to hold the scrap catcher.

8. Finish stuffing with fiberfill, distributing the flax and fiberfill evenly. Blind stitch the opening closed.

9. Place a button on either side of the center and stitch in place.

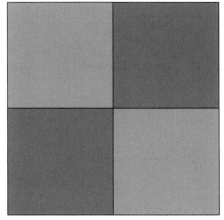

Four Patch.

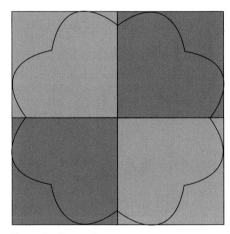

Trace the flower design.

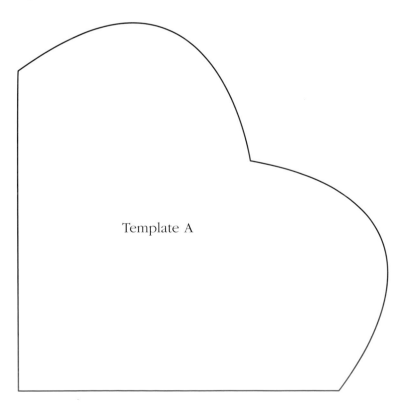

Template A

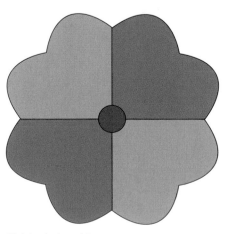

Finished pincushion.

Piecing the Scrap Catcher

1. Fold a 7" x 14" rectangle in half, right sides together. Place the fold at the top.

2. Measure in 1" on the right side of the raw edge along the bottom.

3. Place your ruler on the 1" mark, and align it with the top right corner. Trim. Repeat for other side.

4. Repeat steps 1–3 with the second 7" x 14" rectangle.

5. Place the two trimmed rectangles right sides together. Stitch, leaving a 2" opening.

6. Turn right sides out. Blind stitch the opening closed.

7. Starting with one short end, tuck the bag in on itself. Press.

8. Sew remaining button to inside edge of bag.

Piecing the Connector

1. Hem the short ends of the 2" x 18" strip.

2. Fold lengthwise, right sides together. Stitch ⅛" from long edge. Turn right side out.

3. Press, laying the seam down the back of the strip.

4. Whip stitch the short ends together. Lay flat and press, letting points form at either end.

5. Top stitch across points.

Assembly

Slip one end of the connector strip over the button on the bottom of the pincushion. Slip the other end over the button on the bag. Set near your sewing machine to keep your pins handy and your threads and fabric bits off the floor.

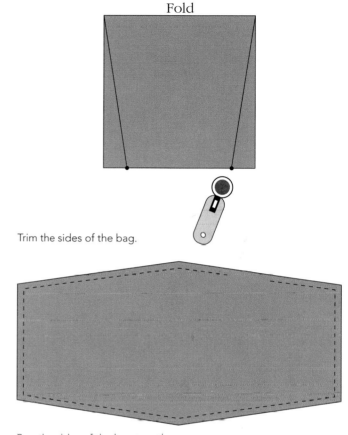

Fold

Trim the sides of the bag.

Sew the sides of the bag together.

Connector strip.

Cream Scones

I've made scones for years, cutting butter into flour—what a mess! Then, one day, I was chatting with Hazel Wolff, a lovely woman who owns Grandmother's Garden Quilt Shop in Hamilton, New Zealand. If her customers call ahead, she'll prepare tea and scones for them! She shared her cream scone recipe with me and that's when I discovered if you use heavy cream, you can skip cutting in the butter and still have a wonderful, flaky scone. With a little experimenting in the kitchen, I've come up with my own version of Cream Scones. I do hope you'll give them a try.

Ingredients

2 cups flour

¼ cup sugar

2 teaspoons baking powder

½ teaspoon salt

1 teaspoon vanilla

1½ cups heavy cream

Note: *Do not substitute half and half or milk for the cream.*

Serves 6

Directions

1. Preheat oven to 400 degrees.

2. Put dry ingredients in a bowl. Whisk to combine.

3. Add vanilla to cream. Stir into dry ingredients. Mix just until a soft dough is formed.

4. Turn out on lightly floured board and knead for 30 seconds. Don't over work dough.

5. Pat into a circle about 1" thick.

6. Cut into six wedges.

7. Bake on parchment lined baking sheet 15–18 minutes until tops are brown but sides are still pale.

Variations

While scones are wonderful plain and topped with butter and jam, a variety of sweet or savory ingredients can be added to the dry mix. Try any of these:

½ cup dried cranberries or blueberries

½ cup grated cheese and 1 teaspoon dried dill

The zest of one lemon and 2 tablespoons poppy seeds

1 cup chocolate chips

THE HERB GARDEN

Whether your herb garden is tucked into a corner of a flower bed just outside the kitchen door; occupies a designated space among the vegetables; or consists of a few pots on a sunny windowsill, a glimpse of those precious herbs hints at culinary delights and tantalizing scents. Enjoy the beauty of an herb garden stitchery, create sachets to tuck into drawers to keep textiles fresh, and impress your family with easy to prepare rosemary potatoes.

Seed Packets Wall Hanging

Pieced and quilted by the author | Wall hanging: 32" x 15" | Block size: 7" x 10"

Have you ever found yourself looking for seeds to plant only to be distracted by the beautiful seed packets themselves? Each individual seed packet can be a work of art. And the names—Blue Ribbon Winner, Harvest Queen, Bumper Crop, Bountiful Harvest—you just know there's a little bit of Farmer's Pride in every packet. Using basic embroidery stitches you can create your own work of art.

Fabric Requirements and Supplies

¼ yd. background fabric

¼ yd. dark fabric for framing

¼ yd. light checkerboard fabric for borders

¼ yd. dark checkerboard fabric for borders

⅝ yd. backing

¼ yd. binding

19" x 36" batting

Freezer paper

Pencil or fine tip water-soluble marker

Crayons

Cutting Instructions

1. From the background fabric, cut:
   3 rectangles 9" x 12" (these will be trimmed later)
2. From the inner border fabric, cut:
   3 strips 1" x 40". Crosscut into 6 strips 1" x 10½" and 6 strips 1" x 8½"
3. From both the light and dark checkerboard fabrics, cut:
   5 strips 1½" x 40"
4. From the binding fabric, cut:
   3 strips 2¼" x 40"

DMC Floss Requirements

Dill

318 No Better

317 Outside border and border around "No Better"

3011 Circle

3012 Stems and leaves

318 Dill Weed

Parsley

334 Ribbon and Blue Ribbon

522 Stems and leaves

936 Parsley

522 Border

Lavender

318 Mist Kissed, Lavender

935 Border around "Lavender"

414 Border around "Mist Kissed"

3011 Leaves

341 Flower stems

793 Flowers

Transferring the Designs

1. Cut a piece of freezer paper the same size as your background fabric.

2. Place the wrong side of the fabric against the shiny side of the freezer paper.

3. With a hot, dry iron, press the fabric to the paper. The wax on the freezer paper will soften and cause the two to stick together. This will stabilize your fabric and make transferring the design and coloring easier.

4. Repeat with the other two background rectangles.

5. Transfer the seed packet designs from page 124 to the background fabric with a pencil or wash out marker.

Coloring and Embroidering Blocks

1. Using crayons, color the designs. Once you have colored the blocks, lay them between two paper towels and press with a dry iron to set the colors.

Note: *Start with a light touch then press. Additional layers of color may be added until the desired depth is achieved. Press between each layer of color.*

2. Thread your needle with two strands of embroidery floss.

3. Use a stem stitch to outline the designs.

4. Use a lazy daisy stitch to form the flowers on the lavender and dill.

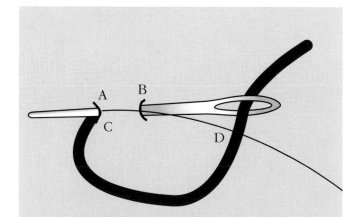

Stem stitch. Work from left to right. Bring needle up at A and down at B. Bring needle up again at C, as close to A as possible. The next stitch starts at D and comes back up at B. Continue bringing the needle up in the same hole as the previous stitch.

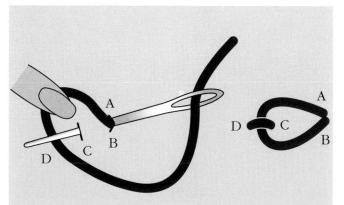

Lazy daisy stitch. Bring the needle up at A. Form a loop of thread and hold it with your thumb. Go down at B, as close to A as possible. Come back up at C and down at D, keeping C and D very close together. To keep an open look to the stitch, don't pull too tightly.

Framing the Blocks

1. Trim embroidered blocks to 7½" x 10½".

2. Add a 10½" framing strip to each side of an embroidered block. Press toward the strip.

3. Add an 8½" framing strip to the top and bottom of the block. Press toward the strip.

4. Repeat with the other two blocks.

Framed block.

Piecing the Borders

1. Sew the light and dark checkerboard fabrics along the long edges.

2. Cut into 108 two-patch segments, 1½" each.

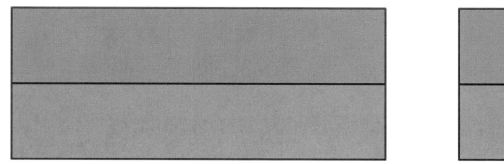

Two-patches.

3. For top and bottom borders, join eight two-patches together to make a set. Make six.

4. Add one set to the top and bottom of each embroidered block.

5. For side borders, join fifteen two-patch blocks together. Make four.

6. Refer to the assembly diagram and join blocks together, being sure to match checkerboard borders with light fabrics touching dark fabrics.

Finishing Your Wall Hanging

1. Prepare your quilt sandwich following the Layering and Basting instructions on page 121.

2. This small wall hanging is the perfect place to try a combination of machine and hand quilting. Machine quilt in the ditch in the checkerboard border, and add some hand quilting in the stitchery blocks.

3. Bind and label following the instructions on page 122.

Assembly diagram.

Double Duty Sachets

Not only do these sachets add a fresh scent to drawers and closets, the combination of cedar chips, herbs, and spices helps keep moths away, too. These sachets also make lovely little gifts for friends. Tie two together with a ribbon for a sweet presentation.

Sachet: 4" x 5"

Fabric Requirements and Supplies

¼ yd. muslin

¼ yd. print fabric

1 cup cedar chips (available in the pet department)

2 tablespoons dried lavender

2 tablespoons dried lemon peel

1 tablespoon whole cloves

Cutting Instructions

To make two sachets

1. From the muslin, cut:
   2 rectangles 5½" x 11"
2. From the print fabric, cut:
   2 rectangles 4½" x 5½"
   4 rectangles 3½" x 5½"

Sewing and Filling the Liner

1. Fold the muslin in half to make a 5½" square.

2. Sew a ¼" seam up each side, creating a little bag. Repeat to make a second bag.

3. Mix the cedar chips, lavender, lemon peel, and cloves in a bowl.

4. Divide the mixture between the two bags.

5. Sew the bag closed. Don't worry about raw edges showing, as this will be tucked into the outer "pillow."

Sewing the Sachet Pillow

1. Hem one 5½" side of each of the 3½" x 5½" rectangles by folding over a ¼", pressing, folding over another ¼", and stitching along the edge of the fold.

2. With right sides together, lay the two hemmed rectangles over a 4½" x 5½" rectangle. The hemmed edges will overlap in the center and raw edges will meet.

3. Stitch using a ¼" seam allowance on all four sides. Trim corners.

4. Turn right sides out. Repeat to make second pillow.

5. Insert muslin bag.

Note: *This is a perfect way to use up small bits of fabric that are just too pretty to throw away. You can use quilting cottons, bark cloth, or brocades. Mix and match them if you'd like.*

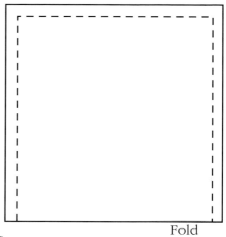

Muslin bag.   Fold

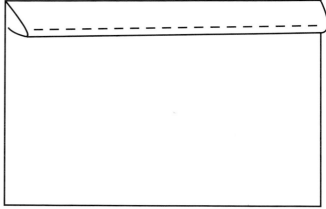

Hemming the edges of the sachet pillow.

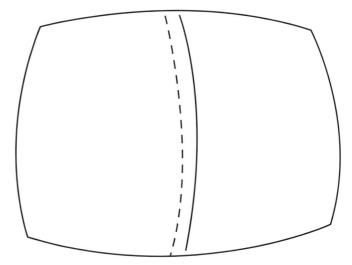

The sachet pillow.

Rosemary Potatoes

A few years ago a group I was a member of was hosting some Lewis and Clark scholars. Shirley Burt brought a wonderfully aromatic potato dish. When I asked for the recipe, she rattled off a list of ingredients with a shrug, assuring me it was simple. I did a little experimenting and discovered she was absolutely correct. This side dish is one of the easiest you'll ever make, but no need to tell your family and guests that! Your kitchen will smell heavenly as these potatoes bake, leaving you time to prepare the rest of the meal or just relax.

Ingredients

8 medium red potatoes
¼ cup olive oil
4 cloves garlic, minced
1 tablespoon dried rosemary, crushed
1 teaspoon salt
½ teaspoon pepper

Serves 8

Preparation

1. Scrub the potatoes and cut into 1½" cubes.

2. Put potatoes in a 9" x 13" baking dish. Drizzle with olive oil. Add remaining ingredients. Toss to coat well.

3. Bake in a preheated 400 degree oven for 30–45 minutes, until potatoes are soft and starting to brown.

THE ORCHARD

The orchard has a way of drawing you in, no matter what the season. As winter draws to an end and the weather begins to warm, the delicate blossoms in springtime offer promises of abundant sweetness. By summer, cherries are ripening and, come fall, bushel baskets will be filled with all colors of apples. An apple core quilt in a variety of reds, yellows, and greens will capture the colors of apple harvest time. The fun blossom coasters serve double duty—they add to the fun factor of a cool drink on a hot day and keep table surfaces protected. Be sure to try the maple apple chicken recipe, too!

Apple Core Quilt

Pieced and quilted by the author | Quilt: 35" x 37½" | Set: 11" x 12"

There is only one shape in this quilt—the apple core. By turning each patch a quarter turn, the blocks interlock, creating a unique design. This is a perfect scrap bag quilt. Gather all your scraps that are the color of apples and create your own apple core quilt.

Fabric Requirements and Supplies

⅛ yd. each six different reds
⅛ yd. each six different yellows
⅛ yd. each six different greens
1⅛ yd. backing
½ yd. binding
40" x 42" batting
Template plastic

Note: *The following items aren't necessary, but will make cutting much easier.*

Acrylic apple core template, available at quilt shops
28-mm rotary cutter
Small rotating cutting mat

Cutting Instructions

If you are using an acrylic template, 28-mm rotary cutter and rotating mat:

1. Cut each ⅛ yard of fabric into eight 5¼" segments.
2. Stack three or four pieces of fabric on the rotating mat. Center template on top.
3. Using the 28-mm rotary cutter, cut around the template, rotating the mat as you go.
4. Continue until you have 144 apple core patches. You will use 132 patches.

Alternate cutting method:

1. Trace a copy of the apple core template on page 39 onto the template plastic. Cut out on traced line.
2. Trace the template 8 times on each ⅛ yard of fabric. Cut out with scissors.

Piecing the Blocks

1. Before beginning, fold each patch in fourths and cut a small notch on all four sides. This notch should not be more than ⅛" deep. The notches will serve as a guide when matching up the patches for sewing.

2. Working on the floor or a design wall lay out the apple core patches, distributing the different colors and prints throughout the quilt. Make twelve rows with eleven blocks in each row.

3. Place two patches, right sides together, matching the notches. Pin.

4. With the concave patch on top, match the ends and pin.

5. Manipulate the convex and concave curves so they match, and continue pinning. Use five to seven pins.

6. Sew with a ¼" seam allowance.

7. Press toward the concave patch.

8. Once the rows are assembled, join them together with partial seams, always sewing with the concave section on top. Pin and sew one patch, then flip the row over, pin and sew the next patch.

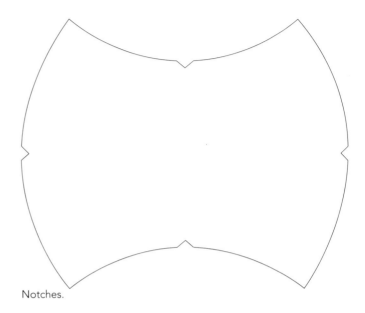

Notches.

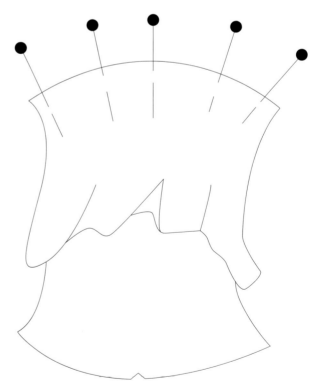

Pinning with the concave patch on top.

Finishing Your Quilt

1. Prepare your quilt sandwich following the Layering and Basting instructions on page 121.

2. The quilt shown was quilted with a red, yellow, and green variegated thread in an all over design.

3. Bind and label following the instructions on page 122.

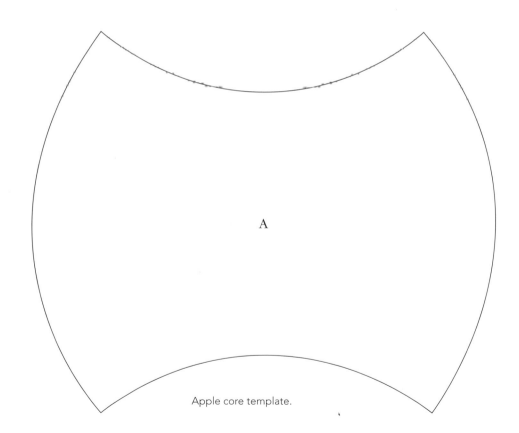

A

Apple core template.

Blossom Coasters

Keep sweaty glasses from leaving rings on your tables with these colorful coasters. They're so fast and fun to make, you can make multiple sets to match all your moods!

Supplies
1 roll of ⅛" thick cork
4 sheets of felt 9" x 12"
Permanent spray adhesive
Template plastic
Craft scissors

Assembly

1. Trace the flower template A and center template B onto template plastic. Cut out with craft scissors.

2. From the cork, cut eight 5" squares.

3. From each sheet of felt, cut two 5" squares.

4. Following the instructions on the spray adhesive, adhere the felt to the cork.

5. Trace the flower shape onto the back (cork side) of the 5" squares. Cut out with craft scissors.

6. From the remaining felt, cut eight flower centers.

7. Mixing the colors, use the spray adhesive to adhere the flower centers to the coasters.

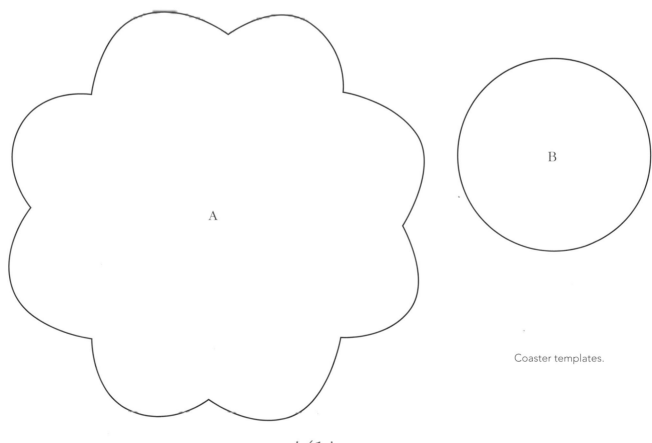

A

B

Coaster templates.

Maple Apple Chicken

Many years ago, I came across a recipe for apple pie that was sweetened with maple syrup. I discovered I really liked the combination and before long had adapted it to this entree. It's a dish that is impressive enough for company, but easy enough to make any night of the week. The combination of tart apples and sweet maple syrup will surprise your palate.

Ingredients

1 medium onion
8 chicken breasts
1 teaspoon salt
½ teaspoon pepper
2 tart green apples
⅓ cup maple syrup

Serves 6

Preparation

1. Slice the onion and spread it across the bottom of a 9" x 13" pan.

2. Place the chicken breasts over the onions. Sprinkle salt and pepper over the meat.

3. Arrange the apples over the top.

4. Drizzle the maple syrup over the chicken breasts and apples.

5. Bake in a preheated 350 degree oven for 30–40 minutes.

THE CONTAINER GARDEN

Container gardening is perfect for turning hard surfaces into lush gardens. The pots, with their many sizes, shapes, and colors, can be as pretty as the plants growing in them. Matching plants to containers can be as much fun as the gardening itself. So pretty are the saucers of bulbs, stately urns with evergreens, and strawberry pots spilling their fruit down their sides. Besides bringing pots of flowers indoors, you can stitch up the flower pots wall hanging for a bit of summer all year long. Keep your pins sharp with an emery strawberry pincushion, and be sure to take advantage of strawberry season with some homemade strawberry shortcake.

Potted Plants Wall Hanging

Pieced by Monica Solorio-Snow and quilted by the author | Wall hanging: 24" x 36" | Block size: 6" x 6"

A combination of piecing and appliqué brings this wall hanging to life. Choose a sweet floral fabric for the border, and let the colors in it determine the color you choose for your flowers. This is the perfect project to bring a little springtime indoors.

Fabric Requirements and Supplies

½ yd. background fabric

⅛ yd. dark brown for pot rim

¼ yd. medium brown for pots

⅛ yd. red flowers

Scrap of yellow for flower centers

¼ yd. green for leaves and stems

⅜ yd. print for borders

⅞ yd. backing fabric

½ yd. for bias binding

Spray-on Fusible Web

Easy Scallop Tool (optional)

Cutting Instructions

Full-size templates can be copied from page 125.

1. From the background fabric, cut:
   2 strips 6½" x 40". Crosscut into 6 squares 6½" x 6½"; 6 rectangles 3½" x 6½"; 6 A and 6 A reversed
2. From the dark brown fabric, cut:
   2 strips 1½" x 40". Crosscut into 6 rectangles 1½" x 6½"
3. From the medium-brown fabric, cut:
   1 strip 6½" x 40". Crosscut into 6 rectangles 5½" x 6½". Trim, using template B as a guide
4. From the red fabric, cut:
   6 C
5. From the yellow fabric, cut:
   6 D
6. From the green fabric, cut:
   1 strip 1¼" x 40". Crosscut into 6 strips 1¼" x 3½" for stems; 12 E

From the border fabric, cut:
   3 strips 3½" x 40"

From the binding fabric, cut:
   6 bias strips 1½" x 40"

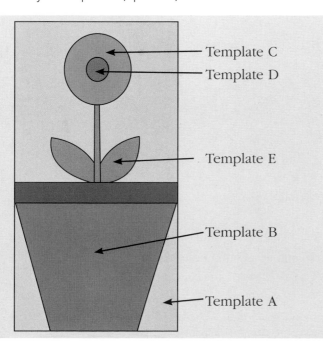

Template C
Template D
Template E
Template B
Template A

Piecing the Blocks
Flower Pots

1. Join an A and AR background piece to each side of pot B

2. Add the dark brown 1½" strip to the top of the pot. Make six.

Flowers

Note: *The flowers and leaves are done with raw edge appliqué. See page 120 for instructions on raw edge appliqué.*

1. Fold a 1¼" x 3½" green stem in half lengthwise, wrong sides together. Finger press.

2. Sew with a scant ¼" seam. Trim seam to ⅛".

3. Center seam on back of strip and press open.

4. Referring to the layout diagram, appliqué stem in place.

5. Next, appliqué the leaves, flower, and flower center.

6. Repeat to make six flower blocks.

Assembling the Top

1. Lay the blocks out in three vertical rows. Rows one and three start with a 3½" x 6½" filler block. Row two ends with a filler block.

2. Sew the blocks in each row together.

3. Join the rows together.

Adding the Borders

1. Measure the width of your quilt crosswise through the middle. This will prevent you from having wavy borders. Mathematically this number would be 18½", but everyone's seam allowances vary, so be sure to measure.

2. Using one of the 3½" strips, cut two strips the width of your quilt.

3. Sew one to the top and bottom of the quilt. Press toward the border.

4. Now measure your quilt lengthwise through the middle. This measurement should be approximately 36½", but check your measurement to be sure.

5. Cut two strips this length.

6. Add them to the sides of your quilt. Press toward the border.

Finishing Your Quilt

1. Prepare your quilt sandwich following the Layering and Basting instructions on page 121.

2. Before quilting, mark the scalloped borders. You can experiment with different size saucers and plates, or use the Easy Scallop Tool. Have fun with your quilting. Quilt clouds in the background, swirls in the border, and squiggles in the pots. Just remember, don't quilt through your appliqués.

3. Bind and label following the instructions for Bias Binding on page 122.

Strawberry Pincushion

Be warned! Making strawberry pincushions can be habit forming. They are so fast and fun to make, and so very adorable, that you'll want to make more and more of them. To keep needles and pins sharp, fill them with emery or sharp sand.

Supplies

Small pieces of felt or tightly woven pink or red
    fabric for strawberries
Green felt scraps for leaves
Embroidery floss
Emery or sharp sand
A small button
Template plastic

Assembly

1. Transfer template shapes to template plastic. Cut out with craft scissors.

2. Trace template A onto back of pink or red fabric. Cut out.

3. Embellish with French knots or lazy daisy stitches (page 26) if desired.

4. Fold the fabric into a cone shape, right sides together.

5. Using an ⅛" seam allowance, stitch together with tiny stitches. Turn right side out.

6. Sew a small running stitch around the open edge, and leave the thread end long for gathering.

7. Fill the cone with emery or sharp sand about three quarters full.

8. Pull the gathering thread tight and secure.

9. From green felt, cut cap with template B.

10. Secure to the top of the strawberry with a few stitches and a button.

To make a French knot, bring floss up at A. Wrap the floss around the needle two times. Hold it firmly, but not too tightly. Insert the needle back into the fabric as close to A as possible, holding the floss and gently pulling the needle through the loops.

Templates.

Strawberry Shortcake

Nothing says summer like strawberries. As busy as we all seem to be in the summer, it's tempting to take the easy way out and buy the little shortcake cups you find at the grocery store. But at least once this season, stir up some homemade shortcakes from scratch. It's easier than you might think. As a young bride, I discovered strawberry shortcake was an easy and impressive dessert. So, take advantage of fresh strawberries this season and bake up a batch of shortcake. Slice ripe strawberries over them and top it all with sweetened whipped cream. It doesn't get much better than that!

Ingredients

Shortcake
2 cups flour

¼ cup sugar

3 teaspoons baking powder

1 teaspoon salt

¼ cup butter

1 teaspoon lemon extract

¾ cup milk

Strawberries
1 quart fresh strawberries

Cream
1 pint whipping cream

2 tablespoons sugar

1 teaspoon vanilla

Serves 8

Preparation

Shortcake

1. Put dry ingredients in a bowl. Stir lightly with a whisk to combine.

2. Cut in butter until mixture looks like coarse meal.

3. Add lemon extract to milk. Mix with dry ingredients until a soft dough forms.

4. Turn out on a lightly floured board. Knead 30 seconds. Do not overwork dough.

5. Roll or press dough until it is about 1" thick.

6. Cut eight 3" round shortcakes.

7. Bake at 425 degrees 10–12 minutes, until just golden brown.

Strawberries

Note: *Prepare the strawberries as close to serving time as possible.*

1. Rinse strawberries under cool, running water.

2. Set aside eight strawberries with hulls still attached for garnish, if desired.

3. Hull and slice berries.

Cream

1. Combine cream, sugar, and vanilla.

2. Whip until soft peaks form.

Assembly

1. Split a shortcake and put the bottom half on a plate.

2. Add a generous amount of strawberries.

3. Cover with the top of the shortcake.

4. Add an even more generous amount of whipped cream!

5. Garnish with a fresh strawberry.

WINDMILLS AND PINWHEELS

What would a garden be without windmills and pinwheels. While not many gardeners rely on a windmill to bring water up from the ground, they still welcome the architectural beauty of these forgotten work horses. Pinwheels bring movement to the garden as well as providing a fun wind accent. Borrow the design of windmill blades to make a striking baby quilt. Enjoy the fun of making pretty pinwheels with your favorite youngsters, and bake up a batch of date pinwheel cookies.

Windmill Blades Baby Quilt

Pieced and quilted by the author | Quilt: 36" x 48" | Block size: 6" x 6"

Simple half-square triangles replicate the spinning blades of a windmill in this baby quilt. Don't limit yourself to soft pastels for baby's quilt. Bold colors, even black and white, are perfect, too!

Fabric Requirements

1½ yd. light #1 for background, border, and binding
⅔ yd. light #2 for setting squares
⅞ yd. dark for windmill blades and flange
1⅓ yd. backing
40" x 52" batting

Cutting Instructions

1. From light #1, cut:
   4 strips 3⅞" x 40". Crosscut into 36 squares 3⅞" x 3⅞" for windmill blades
   4 strips 3½" x 40" for border
   5 strips 2¼" x 40" for binding
2. From light #2, cut
   3 strips 6½" x 40". Crosscut into 17 setting squares 6½" x 6½"
3. From the dark fabric, cut:
   4 strips 3⅞" x 40". Crosscut into 36 squares 3⅞" x 3⅞" for windmill blades
   5 strips 1" x 40" for flange

Piecing the Blocks

To make the half-square triangles:

1. Draw a diagonal line from corner to corner on the wrong side of the light 3⅞" windmill squares.

2. Pair each of these with a 3⅞" dark windmill square.

3. Sew ¼" on either side of the marked line.

4. Cut on the solid line. Press to the darker fabric.

Making the half-square triangles.

5. Sew the half-square triangles into pairs. Sew the pairs into blocks.

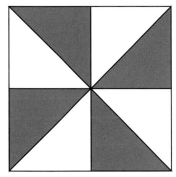

Windmill blocks.

Assembling the Top

1. Working on a design wall or on the floor, lay out the windmill blade blocks and the setting squares. Refer to the layout diagram for the placement.

2. Join the blocks together into rows.

3. Press the seams in each row in toward the setting squares. This will allow the seams in each row to nest with the seams in the row below it.

4. Join the rows together. Press.

Adding the Border

1. Measure the length of your quilt lengthwise through the middle. This will prevent you from having wavy borders. Mathematically, this number would be 42½", but everyone's seam allowances vary, so be sure to measure.

2. Cut two strips the length of your quilt.

3. Attach one to each side of the quilt. Press.

4. Now measure your quilt crosswise through the middle. This measurement should be approximately 36½", but check your measurement to be sure.

5. Cut two strips this length.

6. Attach one to the top and one to the bottom of your quilt. Press.

Finishing Your Quilt

1. Prepare your quilt sandwich following the Layering and Basting instructions on page 121.

2. Machine stippling is a nice finish for a baby quilt that is likely to be washed many times. If you leave the dark areas of the windmill blades unquilted, they will stand out from the rest of the quilt.

Adding the Flange

1. Join the 1" strips together with diagonal seams. Press seams open.

2. Press the flange strip lengthwise, wrong sides together.

3. Align the raw edges of the strip with one side of the quilt. Sew with a scant ¼" seam. Trim flange even with the end of the quilt.

4. Repeat with the opposite side, then the top and bottom of the quilt. The binding should cover your stitches.

5. Bind and label following the instructions on page 122

Layout diagram.

Pretty Pinwheels

Remember how much fun you had as a child when you held a pinwheel in the wind or ran across the yard to see how fast you could make it spin? Pass the joy on to someone you love with this fun craft project or make some just for decoration.

Supplies

For one pinwheel

2 scraps of fabric 6"

6" square heavy duty fusible web such as Heat and
  Bond Ultra

Pushpin

¼" dowel, 12" long

Assembly

1. Fuse the two squares of fabric together following manufacturer's instructions.

2. Draw diagonal lines from corner to corner on one side of the fabric.

3. Measure in 3" from each outside corner and mark with a dot.

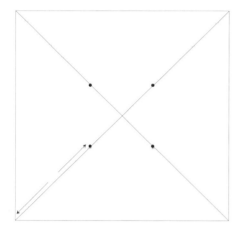

Marking

4. Cut along marked lines, stopping at the dots.

5. Bring every other point to the center and stick the pushpin through all four points, being sure pin goes through exact center.

6. Wiggle the pin a bit to enlarge the hole, so the pinwheel will spin freely.

7. Stick the pin into the dowel and have fun!

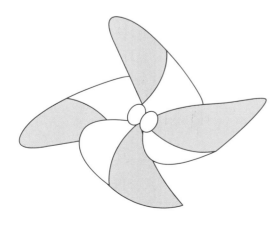

Date Pinwheel Cookies

I was introduced to Date Pinwheel Cookies the first time I accompanied my husband to Montana for Christmas. They were a tradition in his family and his mother made big batches of them. Now it's up to me to carry on that tradition, and while I make them with enthusiasm, I can never get them to look as perfectly round as she did. No matter what their shape, we still enjoy the combination of sweet, soft dates, finely chopped walnuts, and brown-sugar cookie dough that make this cookie unique.

Ingredients

4 cups flour
½ teaspoon salt
½ teaspoon baking soda
1 cup butter
2 cups brown sugar
3 eggs, beaten
2¼ cups chopped dates
1 cup sugar
1 cup finely chopped walnuts
1 cup water

Preparation
Cookie Dough

1. Combine first three ingredients. Stir with a whisk to combine.

2. In another bowl, cream the butter and brown sugar until light and fluffy.

3. Add the eggs and mix two minutes.

4. Add the dry ingredients a little at a time, mixing well.

5. Divide the dough into three equal balls. Wrap in plastic wrap and refrigerate one hour.

Filling

1. Bring dates, sugar, walnuts, and water to a simmer in a small saucepan. Cook ten minutes. Set aside to cool.

Making the Cookies

1. On a lightly floured board, roll out one ball of cookie dough into a 12" x 8" rectangle.

2. Spread a third of the date filling evenly on the dough.

3. Beginning with the long side, roll the dough up jelly roll style.

4. Wrap in plastic wrap and refrigerate over night.

5. Repeat with the other two balls of dough.

6. With a thin, sharp knife, slice rolls into ¼" thick slices.

7. Place 1" apart on cookie sheet.

8. Bake at 375 degrees for 8–10 minutes.

THE VEGETABLE GARDEN

This most utilitarian of gardens has a beauty in its own right. It's a joy to see stately rows of carrot tops swaying in the wind, plump heads of cabbage wrapped in coats of oversized leaves, and pea vines racing up their supports. The vegetable garden must have inspired quilters long ago to come up with the pattern for corn and beans, which we recreate here as a table runner. The garden also inspired our embroidered tea towels and the sweet and tangy corn relish.

Corn-and-Beans Table Runner

Pieced by Melinda Crowley and quilted by the author | Table runner: 16" x 40" | Block size: 12" x 12"

It only takes three corn-and-bean blocks to make this runner—it's the addition of a pieced border that gives it a unique look. Let a runner like this brighten your summer table.

Fabric Requirements

¾ yd. background fabric

1¼ yd. yellow

⅞ yd. green

⅝ yd. backing

20" x 44" batting

Cutting Instructions

1. From the background fabric, cut:
   2 strips 4⅞" x 40". Crosscut into 9 squares 4⅞" x 4⅞". Cut each square once diagonally to make 18 triangles.
   5 strips 2⅞" x 40". Crosscut into 38 squares 2⅞" x 2⅞". Cut each square once diagonally to make 76 triangles.
   2 strips 2½" x 40". Crosscut each strip into 6 pieces 4½" x 2½" and 2 pieces 6½" x 2½".
2. From the yellow fabric, cut:
   2 strips 2⅞" x 40". Crosscut Into 18 squares 2⅞" x 2⅞". Cut each square once diagonally to make 36 triangles.
3. From the green fabric, cut:
   1 strip 5¼" x 40". Crosscut into 5 squares 5¼" x 5¼". Crosscut each square twice diagonally to make 20 triangles.
   1 strip 4⅞" x 40". Crosscut into 3 squares 4⅞" x 4 ⅞". Cut each square once diagonally to make 6 triangles.
   3 strips 2¼" x 40" for binding.

Piecing the Blocks

1. Make a flying geese unit by adding a 2⅞" background triangle to each side of a small green triangle. Make twenty.

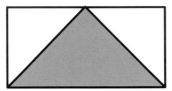

Flying geese. Make 20.

2. Set aside eight flying geese units for the border. To the remaining twelve flying geese units, add a yellow triangle on each end.

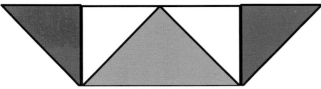

Make 12.

3. Join a 2⅞" background triangle to a 2⅞" yellow triangle. Make twelve.

Make 12.

4. Add a 2⅞" triangle to each side of the unit made in Step 3.

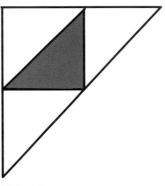

Make 12.

5. Add a 4⅞" green triangle to a unit made in Step 4.

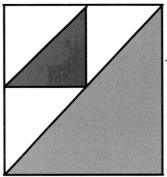

Make 6.

6. Add a 4⅞" background triangle to a unit made in Step 4. Make six.

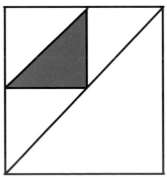

Make 6.

7. Assemble the units into three corn-and-bean blocks.

Corn-and-bean block. Make 3.

Piecing the Borders

1. Add a 2½" x 4½" rectangle of background fabric to each side of a flying geese unit. Make 6.

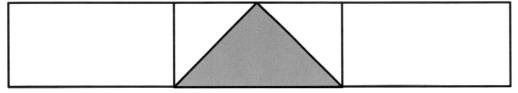

Make 6.

2. Add a 2½" x 6½" rectangle background fabric to each side of a flying geese unit. Make 2.

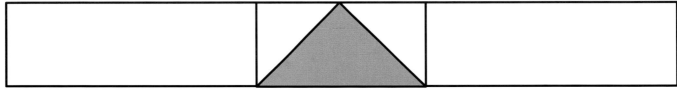

Make 2.

Assembling the Top

1. Add a short border unit to two sides of a corn-and-beans block. Repeat with all three blocks.

2. Join the three blocks together.

3. Add a long border unit to each side of the runner.

Finishing Your Table Runner

1. Prepare your quilt sandwich following the Layering and Basting instructions on page 121.

2. Machine quilting in the ditch is an easy and appropriate finish for this table runner.

3. Bind and label following the instructions on page 122.

Layout diagram.

Garden Inspired Tea Towels

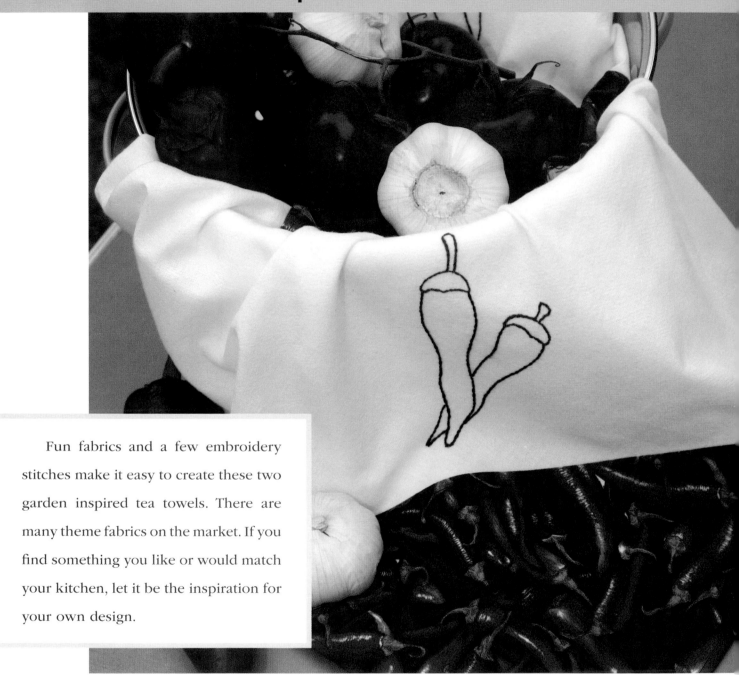

Fun fabrics and a few embroidery stitches make it easy to create these two garden inspired tea towels. There are many theme fabrics on the market. If you find something you like or would match your kitchen, let it be the inspiration for your own design.

Supplies

Two tea towels

⅜ yd. fruit or vegetable themed fabric or a scrap at least 12" x 12"

1 package ¼" fusible web such as Steam-A-Seam

Floss to match the design

Cutting Instructions

1. Cut a 12" x 12" square of fabric
2. Cut in half diagonally.

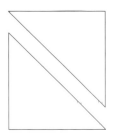

Cutting the fabric.

Sewing

1. Press under ¼" on the diagonal edge of the fabric. Take care not to stretch the bias edge.

2. Cut a strip of ¼" fusible web approximately 17" long and apply to pressed edge.

3. Turn under another ¼", press to fuse.

4. Press under ¼" on each remaining side.

5. Lay a corner of the tea towel over the fabric triangle. Let the fabric triangle extend ¼" beyond the towel.

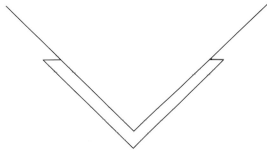

Placement

6. Cut a 12" strip of the ¼" fusible web and apply to pressed edge.

7. Turn under another ¼" and press to the edge of the towel.

8. Repeat with remaining edge.

9. Top stitch all three sides with matching thread.

Embroidery

1. Trace the embroidery design onto the tea towel with a pencil or fine tip water soluble marker.

Note: *You may want to choose a design that matches the fabric you are using. Try isolating a section of the image from the fabric itself.*

2. Embroider the designs with a stem stitch. See page 26.

3. Repeat to make second tea towel.

Corn Relish

My Grandma Kennedy was a farm girl and a farm wife, and her cooking reflected that lifestyle. Good country fare was her claim to fame, and no one ever left her house hungry. I remember corn relish as being a homey, country concoction that I never thought would grace the table of a fine restaurant or the pages of a contemporary cuisine magazine, but all that seems to have changed. Today, corn relish has achieved fine-dining status. It is great served as an appetizer on crostini, as a sandwich condiment, mixed into a pasta salad or as a dip with tortilla chips. The flavor of this tasty relish improves after a few days in the refrigerator, but if you can't wait, it's okay to have some right away! Consider making it for gifts, too.

Ingredients

(4) 12 ounce cans of whole kernel corn

1 cup vinegar

1 cup sugar

1 teaspoon celery salt

4 ounce jar pimentos, chopped

4 ounce can jalapeño peppers, chopped

Preparation

1. Drain two cans of the corn. Leave the liquid in the other two.

2. In a saucepan, heat vinegar, sugar and celery salt to a boil. Boil 2 minutes.

3. Remove from heat. Stir in remaining ingredients.

4. Cool. Ladle into jars, if desired. Refrigerate up to two weeks.

GARDEN TRELLIS

A garden trellis is a pretty sight to see. It brings the flowers up from ground level and overhead. The structure itself is usually a work of art in its own right, with elegant supports and lattice for the vines to cling to. The double Irish chain quilt echoes the lattice found in a trellis, as does the woven ribbon in the eyeglass case. Pretty crust on the lattice top cranberry apple pie lets the fruit peek through to tempt you.

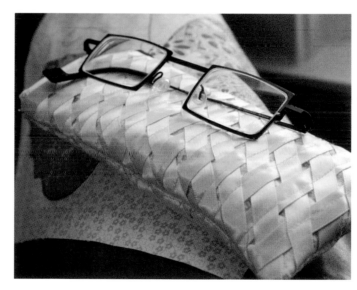

Double Irish Chain Quilt

Pieced by Janet King and quilted by the author | Quilt: 62" x 82" | Block size: 10" x 10"

Once you learn the secrets of strip piecing, this quilt is a breeze to make. You only need to choose three colors for this traditional pattern. The large background squares give you plenty of space for some special quilting.

Fabric Requirements

3¾ yd. blue
2½ yd. green
1¼ yd. yellow floral
4¾ yd. backing
66" x 82" batting

Cutting Instructions

1. From the blue fabric, cut:
   22 strips 2½" x 40" (set aside 15 strips for borders)
   6 strips 6½" x 40", crosscut into 17 rectangles 6½" x 10½".
   8 strips 2¼" x 40" for binding
2. From the green fabric, cut:
   32 strips 2½" x 40" (set aside 7 strips for border)
3. From the floral fabric, cut:
   14 strips 2½" x 40".

Piecing the Blocks
Block A

Note: *There are three strip sets that make up block A.*
Strip set #1—floral, green, blue, green, floral.
Strip set #2—green, floral, green, floral, green.
Strip set #3—blue, green, floral, green, blue.

1. Make three of strip set #1.

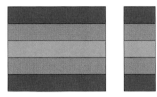

Strip set #1.

2. Make three of strip set #2.

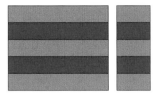

Strip set #2.

3. Make two of strip set #3.

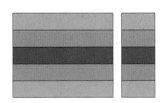

Strip set #3.

4. Press all seams toward the green fabric.

5. Crosscut strip sets 1 and 2 into thirty-six 2½" segments.

6. Crosscut both #3 strip sets into eighteen 2½" segments.

7. Lay out the segments as shown in the block diagram. Nest seams together and join to make completed Block A. Make 18.

Block A.

Block B

1. Join a 2½" green strip to both sides of a 6½" blue strip. Repeat to make two strip sets.

Piecing strip sets.

2. Crosscut strip sets into thirty-four 2½" segments.

3. Sew a segment to each side of a 6½" x 10½" rectangle.

Block B.

Assembling the Top

1. Lay the blocks out in seven rows of five blocks. Begin with an A block in the upper left hand corner and alternate A and B blocks.

2. Join the blocks together into rows.

3. Press the seams in each row toward the B blocks. This will allow the seams in each row to nest with the seams in the row below it.

4. Join the rows together. Press.

Adding the Borders

1. Join the blue strips for the inner and outer borders together by sewing diagonal seams. Press. Join all of the strips together until you have one long strip.

2. Measure the length of your quilt lengthwise through the middle. This will prevent you from having wavy borders. Mathematically, this number would be 70½" but everyone's seam allowances vary, so be sure to measure.

3. Cut two strips the length of your quilt.

4. Attach one to each side of the quilt. Press.

5. Now measure your quilt crosswise through the middle. This measurement should be approximately 54½" but check your measurement to be sure.

6. Cut two strips this length.

7. Add them to the top and bottom of your quilt. Press.

8. Repeat steps 1–7 with the green center border strips.

9. Repeat steps 2–7 with the outer blue border.

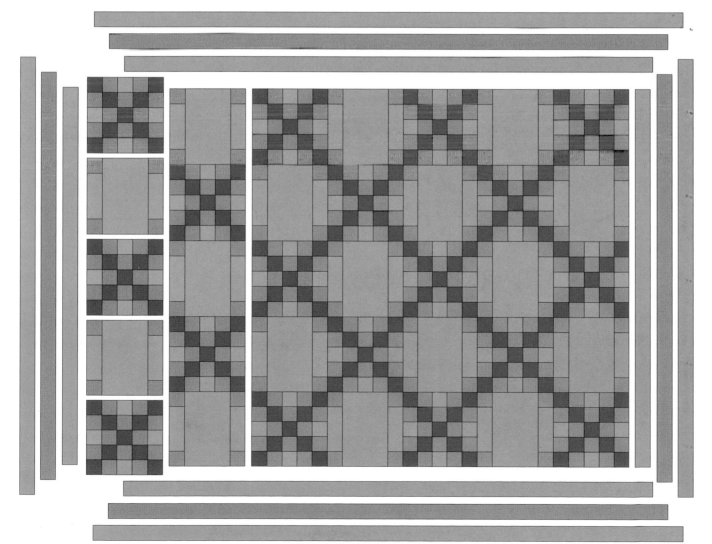

Layout diagram.

Woven Eyeglass Case

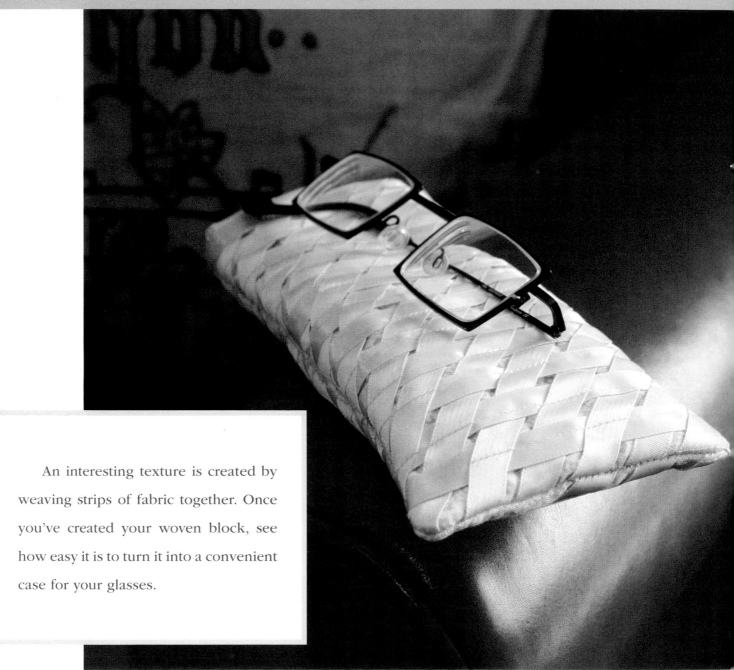

An interesting texture is created by weaving strips of fabric together. Once you've created your woven block, see how easy it is to turn it into a convenient case for your glasses.

Fabric Requirements

¼ yd. muslin or fabric to match your ribbon

5 yd. ribbon (⅜")

Batting scrap at least 7½" square

Cutting Instructions

From the muslin, cut:
  1 strip 7½" x 40". Crosscut into 1 square 7½" x 7½" and 1 rectangle 7½" x 8" for lining.

From the ribbon, cut:
  13 strips, 8" x ⅜"

Note: *Diagonal strips will be cut as you do the weaving.*

Ribbon Weaving

1. Pin thirteen pieces of ribbon horizontally across the 7½" square, leaving ½" at the top and bottom.

Spacing the ribbon strips.

2. Using a scant ¼" seam, stay stitch the ends of the ribbon to the square.

3. Weave the remaining ribbon at a diagonal through the ribbons stitched to the square. Start in one corner, pinning the ribbon in place and cutting to length as you work

Weaving the diagonal ribbons.

4. Using a scant ¼" seam, stay stitch the ends of the ribbon to the square.

5. Top stitch all of the horizontal ribbons.

Assembling the Eyeglass Case

1. Layer the lining and woven square, right sides together. Place a 7½" square of batting on top. Stitch one edge with a ¼" seam allowance. Open and press toward the lining.

2. Fold in half lengthwise, right sides together. Stitch the long side and the end with the weaving.

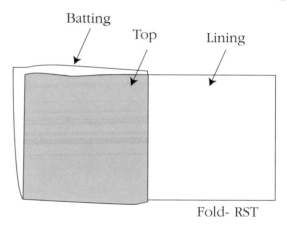

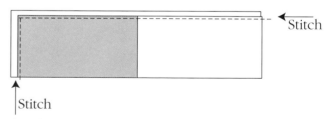

Stitching the eyeglass case.

3. Trim corners and turn right sides out.

4. Turn ¼" of the open edge of the lining in and press. Top stitch.

5. Starting with the short end of the lining, tuck the bag in on itself. Press.

Lattice Top Cranberry Apple Pie

When my grandma, mom, and aunts would get together to make pies, it wasn't just two or three pies. I remember one time when we spent the afternoon together and made 100 pies! Grandma was famous for her pie crust, and when I finally did pin her down to get a recipe, she started with "Sixteen cups of flour, a handful of salt ...." Her recipe made enough dough for nine double-crust pies! I've whittled the pie-crust recipe down in case you're not inclined to make that many pies at one time.

My husband and I are one of about thirty families in this area who farm cranberries, and we love to incorporate this tart, red fruit into many of our meals. Here, cranberries combine with another favorite fall fruit—apples—in a luscious pie. If you plan ahead and put some cranberries in the freezer next fall, you can enjoy this pie all year 'round

Ingredients

Crust

2½ cups flour

1 teaspoon salt

1 cup butter

¼—½ cup water

Filling

3 cups fresh or frozen cranberries

1 cup water

1½ cups sugar

¼ cup corn starch

¼ teaspoon cinnamon

¼ teaspoon cloves

2 cups apples, peeled, and sliced

Preparation

Crust

1. Cut butter into small pieces, approximately ½".

2. Combine butter, flour, and salt in a food processor.

3. Pulse until mixture resembles coarse meal.

4. With food processor running, slowly add between ¼ cup and ½ cup water, until mixture comes together into a ball of dough.

5. Divide the dough into two flat disks, about 6" across. Wrap in plastic wrap and refrigerate at least one hour.

Filling

1. In a saucepan, combine cranberries and water. Bring to a boil. Simmer three minutes.

2. Mix sugar, cornstarch, and spices to blend. Add to boiling mixture.

3. Stir constantly until mixture thickens. Cook thirty seconds then remove from heat.

Note: *If desired, remove some berries and set aside for garnishing the pie after it bakes.*

4. Stir in apples and set aside while you prepare the crust.

Assembly

1. Roll out one disk of pie dough and place in a 9" pie pan. Let ½" dough hang over the edge.

2. Roll out remaining dough into a 10" circle. Cut ½" wide strips.

3. Lay strips in one direction over top of pie, leaving 1" space between strips.

4. Fold back alternate strips and weave additional strips across. Trim lattice even with the edge of lower pie crust.

5. Fold lower crust over the lattice. Crimp.

6. Bake in a 400 degree oven 35–45 minutes.

Delicious served with cinnamon ice cream!

BIRDS, BEES, AND BUTTERFLIES

What garden would be complete without birds, bees, and butterflies. Besides bringing joy to those who visit the garden, these creatures have a duty to perform to keep our gardens healthy and growing. Many gardeners do all they can to attract birds, bees, and butterflies to the garden. You can pay tribute to the ethereal butterfly by making either a butterfly quilt-in-a-pillow or a butterfly potholder. And then let the labor of the bees sweeten your raspberry honey milkshake.

Butterfly Quilt-in-a-Pillow

Pieced by Janet King and quilted by the author | Quilt: 42" x 70"

Here's a snuggly quilt and pillow all in one. When you need a blanket to toss over you, this quilt is just the right size. When not in use, fold it into a square and pop it into the attached pillowcase. Perfect for on the couch, in the car, or at a picnic.

Fabric Requirements

½ yd. fabric for the pillowcase

10"–12" pieced quilt block or "cheater" fabric (optional)

2 yd. fabric for quilt top

2 yd. fabric for quilt back

20" square of batting

46" x 74" batting

Cutting Instructions

1. From the pillowcase fabric, cut:
   2 squares 18½" x 18½"

Note: *If using a quilt block, add borders around the block to make the finished size 18½". Use this block in place of one of the 18½" squares. The sample was made with a preprinted butterfly block, but we've included the pattern if you'd like to reproduce it by hand.*

2. Trim the selvage from the top and backing pieces.

Piecing the Blocks

Pillowcase

1. Lay out the 20" square of batting. Place the quilt block or one 18½" square of fabric on top of the batting, right sides up. Place another 18½" square of fabric wrong side up. Pin all edges of the three layers.

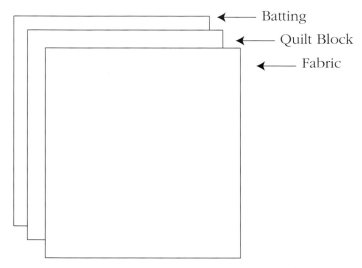

Batting

Quilt Block

Fabric

Pillowcase.

2. Using a ¼" seam allowance, sew around all four sides of pillowcase, leaving a 6"–8" opening along one side for turning.

3. Trim excess batting and bulk at corners.

4. Reach in between the two layers of fabric and turn the pillowcase right sides out. Press.

5. Close the opening with a blind stitch.

6. Quilt by hand or machine to hold batting in place.

Quilt

1. On a large, flat surface, lay out the batting, top fabric right side up and backing fabric, wrong side up. Pin all four edges.

2. Using a ¼" seam allowance, sew around all four sides of the quilt, leaving a 10"–12" opening along one side for turning.

3. Trim excess batting and bulk at corners.

4. Reach in between the two layers of fabric and turn the quilt right sides out. Press.

5. Machine quilt or tie the quilt.

Assembling the Top

1. Find the center of the top of the pillow case. Mark with a pin.

2. Find the center of one short side of the quilt. Mark with a pin.

3. Matching the pins, put the pillowcase right side down on the back of the quilt. Pin in place.

4. Stitch three sides of the pillowcase to the quilt, reinforcing the ends with extra stitches.

Note: *Do not stitch across the bottom of the pillowcase.*

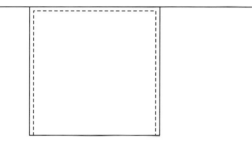

Placement of the pillowcase.

Folding the Quilt-in-a-Pillow

1. With the backing facing up, fold the quilt into thirds lengthwise.

2. Now fold the length in half, then in half again, bringing the bottom toward the top.

3. Pull the pillowcase over the folded quilt.

Folded quilt-in-a-pillow.

Butterfly Potholder

The potholder is the workhorse of the kitchen. There's no reason for it to be ordinary, though. Take a few minutes to appliqué a butterfly to a piece of fabric and stitch it into a pretty potholder

Fabric Requirements

⅝ yd. background
2 scraps floral print for butterflies, at least 9" x 9"
Scrap of solid fabric for butterfly body
Fusible spray
Floss
2 squares batting, 14"
Basting spray

Cutting Instructions

1. From the background fabric, cut:
   3 strips 2¼" x 40" for binding
   4 squares 12" x 12"
2. From the print fabrics, cut:
   2 butterflies (Template A)
3. From the solid fabric, cut:
   2 bodies (Template B)

Appliquéing the Butterflies

Note: *The butterflies are done with raw edge appliqué. See page 121 for instructions on raw edge appliqué.*

1. Appliqué one butterfly to a background square.

2. Repeat with second butterfly.

3. Use embroidery floss to finish the edges and add details.

Making the Potholders

1. Working in a well ventilated area, spray the wrong side of a background square with basting spray.

2. Smooth a square of batting over the backing.

3. Spray the wrong side of a butterfly block with basting spray. Place over batting.

4. Hand or machine quilt around the butterfly. Trim to 11".

5. Repeat with second block.

6. Bind edges, adding a loop if desired.

Raspberry Honey Milkshake

When my mom graduated from high school in the small town of Raymond, Washington, she decided to open a luncheonette. She served hamburgers, milkshakes, and homemade pies--thanks to Grandma. Grandma also surprised her by presenting her with a brand new Hamilton Beach milkshake mixer to help get the new business off to a quick start. Growing up, I remember the mixer at my aunt and uncle's house. Now it resides in my kitchen. I wonder how many milkshakes that old machine has blended together?

A milkshake is still a welcome treat on a warm summer day, or in the evening while watching a good movie. The addition of a little honey to the fresh raspberries in this version gives the milkshake an unexpected, complex flavor.

Ingredients

1 pint vanilla ice cream
1 cup milk
1 pint fresh raspberries
2 tablespoons honey

Serves 4

Preparation

Note: *Reserve a few raspberries for garnish.*

1. Put all ingredients into a milk shake mixer or food processor.

2. Blend for about 3 minutes.

3. Pour into chilled glasses and serve.

THE SEASIDE GARDEN

The lawn at my childhood home sloped down to the sand dunes where clipped green grass gave way to clumps of beach grass. Gardening in such an environment can be challenging, but in the hands of a dedicated gardener the results can be lovely. Hardy plants that can survive constant breezes and ocean mists offer rewards of variegated foliage and pretty blossoms.

Beach Blanket Bingo

Pieced and quilted by the author | Quilt: 62" x 82" | Block size: 10" x 10"

Here's the perfect quick quilt to make for those summer days on the beach. Leave it in the back of your car and it will always be at the ready for an impromptu picnic or dip in the water. You can spread it on the ground to sit on, or wrap up in it as the evening starts to chill the air. Fun fabrics, simple squares and an occasional snowball block give this quilt visual interest.

Fabric Requirements

12 fat quarters
⅓ yd. fabric for snowball corners
¼ yd. inner border
1⅓ yd. outer border
3⅔ yd. backing
½ yd. binding
66" x 82" batting

Cutting Instructions

Note: *Lay the 18" side of the fat quarter along the bottom edge of the cutting mat, selvage to the top.*

1. From each fat quarter, cut:
   2 strips, 6½" x 40"; crosscut into 6 squares, 6½" x 6½"
2. From the snowball fabric, cut:
   3 strips 2½" x 40"; crosscut into 48 squares, 2½" x 2½"
3. From the inner border fabric, cut:
   6 strips, 1½" x 40"
4. From the outer border fabric, cut:
   7 strips, 6½" x 40"
5. From the binding fabric, cut:
   7 strips, 2¼" x 40"

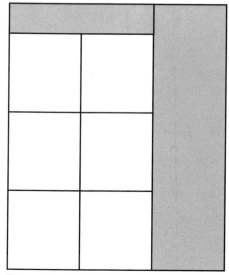

Fat quarter cutting diagram.

Piecing the Blocks

1. Select one 6½" square of each print to make into a snowball block.

2. Draw a diagonal line on the wrong side of the 2½" squares.

3. Carefully place a 2½" square on one corner of a 6½" square, right sides together.

4. Stitch on drawn line.

6. Trim all four corners, leaving a ¼" seam allowance.

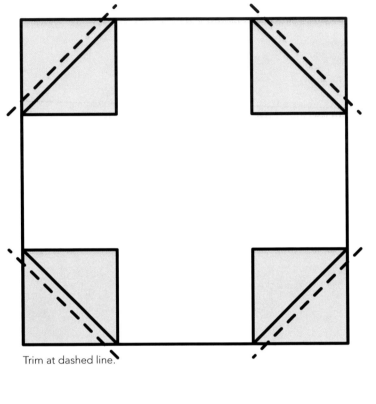

Trim at dashed line.

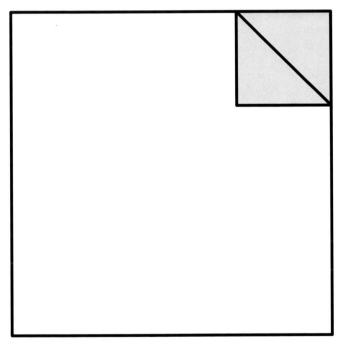

Adding the snowball corners.

5. Repeat, adding a 2½" square to the remaining three corners.

7. Press snowball corners.

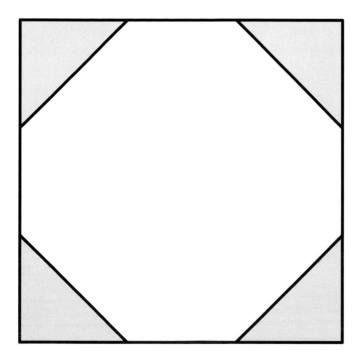

8. Repeat with remaining 6" squares.

Assembling the Top

1. Working on a design wall or on the floor, lay out the 6½" squares in nine rows of eight blocks each. Lay them out in a random fashion, dispersing the snowball blocks evenly throughout. Remember, this is a scrappy quilt, so anything goes, but you will want to avoid having two like fabrics touching.

2. Once you have the blocks laid out in a pleasing manner, join the blocks together into rows.

3. Press the seams in each row in opposite directions. This will allow the seams in each row to nest with the seams in the row below it.

4. Join the rows together. Press.

Adding the Borders

1. Join the strips for the inner border together by sewing diagonal seams. Press open. Join all of the strips together until you have one long strip.

2. Measure the length of your quilt lengthwise through the middle. This will prevent you from having wavy borders. Mathematically this number would be 54½", but everyone's seam allowances vary, so be sure to measure.

3. Cut two strips the length of your quilt.

4. Attach one to each side of the quilt. Press.

5. Now measure your quilt crosswise through the middle. This measurement should be approximately 50½", but check your measurement to be sure.

6. Cut two strips this length.

7. Add them to the top and bottom of your quilt. Press.

8. Repeat steps 1–7 with your outer border fabric.

Finishing Your Quilt

1. Cut your backing fabric into two equal pieces. Remove selvages and join together.

2. Prepare your quilt sandwich following the Layering and Basting instructions on page 121.

3. This quilt is meant for fun, so why not have fun with the quilting, too? In keeping with the theme of this quilt, a pantograph of seashells and fish was used, but loops and stars would make a fine finish.

4. Bind and label following the instructions for Straight of Grain, Double Fold Binding on page 122.

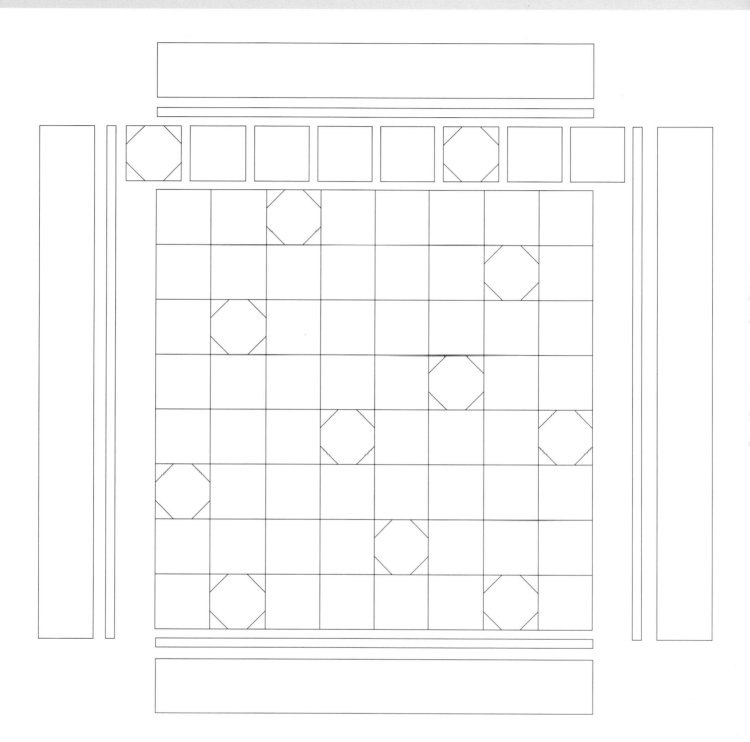

Beach Tote

Here's the perfect beach tote—and it's reversible! It's the perfect size to take to the beach with your towel, sunscreen, and a good book. You'll want to make one for every member of the family.

Fabric Requirements

1½ yd. fabric
¾ yd. cording (¼")
6 grommets

Cutting Instructions

1. From the fabric, cut:
   2 circles, 12½" diameter
   1 rectangle, 36 x 39½"

Piecing the Tote

1. Place the two circles right sides together. Stitch, using a ¼" seam. Leave a 5" opening to turn.

2. Turn right sides out. Press and blind stitch opening together.

3. Fold the rectangle in half, right sides together, to make a 39½" x 18" rectangle.

Rectangle.

4. Stitch raw edges together using a ¼" seam. Leave a 5" opening to turn.

5. Turn right sides out. Press and blind stitch opening together.

6. Form the rectangle into a tube by lapping the two short ends over each other ½". Pin. It is important that the circle and tube fit together perfectly. At this point check the fit and adjust the overlap of the tube if necessary.

7. With a zigzag stitch, top stitch both edges of the tube.

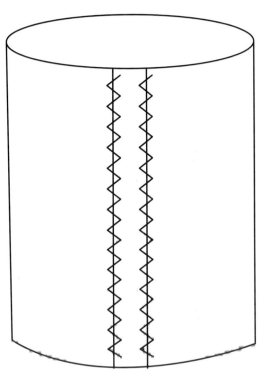

Tube.

8. Butt the circle to the bottom of the tube, and, with a short zigzag stitch, join them together.

9. Add grommets to the top of the bag, spacing evenly.

10. Thread cording through the grommet, tie the ends together and you're ready to fill your bag and head to the beach!

S'mores Cookie Bars

S'mores are a seaside favorite. Roasting marshmallows over a driftwood fire until golden brown, then squishing them between two graham crackers and adding a square of chocolate was always the end to a perfect day at the beach. If you want that yummy taste even when you aren't at the beach, stir up a batch of S'mores Cookie Bars and savor the sweet treat any time.

My sister was still in high school back in 1974 when I got married. As a gift to me she went through Mom's recipes and started a box of family favorites to start me off in my married life. As it turned out, they were all her favorites! It's still the core of my recipe collection, and I treasure the hand written note from her which is still in the front of the box. This recipe for S'mores Cookies is adapted from one of her favorites.

Ingredients

1 cup butter
2½ cups graham cracker crumbs
1 bag milk chocolate chips, 12 oz
1 can sweetened condensed milk, 14 oz
4 cups miniature marshmallows

Preparation

1. Melt butter in a large pan.

2. Stir in graham cracker crumbs. Reserve ½ cup mixture.

3. Press remaining mixture into the bottom of a 9" x 13" pan to form a crust.

4. Cover crust with chocolate chips.

5. Evenly cover with condensed milk.

6. Top with marshmallows.

7. Sprinkle remaining graham cracker mixture over the top.

8. Bake in a 350-degree oven 30–40 minutes.

9. Cool and cut into squares.

WOODLAND GARDEN

We often think of gardens as cultivated spaces, but there is really no better gardener than Mother Nature herself. One of my favorite ways to spend a Sunday afternoon is on a picnic, dining in the shade of big evergreen trees. Filtered sunlight that makes its way to the forest floor nurtures soft mosses and delicate ferns, and each spring the woods near my home offers delicate blossoms including trillium, miner's lettuce, fox gloves and lily-of-the-valley. There's no better garden than that!

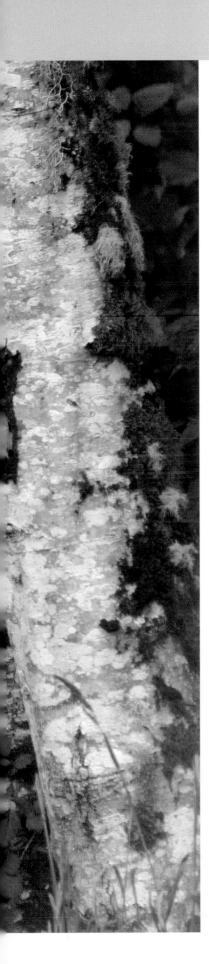

Family Tree Signature Quilt

Pieced and quilted by the author | Quilt: 79" x 90" | Block size: 9" x 9"

At your next family gathering, take the opportunity to collect signatures for a very special heirloom quilt. If you have time, you can make the blocks early and have them ready for signing. If not, take squares of plain fabric and a permanent pen and incorporate them into your quilt at a later date.

For this quilt, I chose a unique border treatment—the top and bottom have four borders, the sides have two borders.

Fabric Requirements

1½ yd. background fabric
2⅔ yd. green print
1⅜ yd. yellow print
1¼ yd. yellow for lattice
2½ yd. solid green
5¼ yd. backing
83" x 94" batting

Cutting Instructions

1. From background fabric, cut:
     5 strips, 3⅞" x 40"; crosscut into 52 squares, 3⅞" x 3⅞"
     3 strips, 4" x 40"; crosscut into 26 squares, 4" x 4". Cut each square in half diagonally for stems.
     5 strips, 3½" x 40"; crosscut into 52 squares, 3½" x 3½"

2. From the green print fabric, cut:
     3 strips, 3⅞" x 40"; crosscut into 26 squares, 3⅞" x 3⅞"
     5 strips, 2" x 40"; crosscut into 26 squares, 2" x 2" and 13 rectangles, 2" x 6½"
     3 strips, 3½" x 40"; crosscut into 26 squares, 3½" x 3½"
     9 strips, 6½" x 40" for the outer border

3. From the yellow print fabric, cut:
     3 strips, 3⅞" x 40"; crosscut into 26 squares, 3⅞" x 3⅞"
     5 strips, 2" x 40"; crosscut into 26 squares, 2" x 2" and 13 rectangles, 2" x 6½"
     3 strips, 3½" x 40"; crosscut into 26 squares, 3½" x 3½"
     4 strips, 3½" x 40" for top and bottom filler border

4. From yellow lattice fabric, cut:
     4 strips, 9½" x 40"; crosscut into 16 squares, 9½" x 9½"

5. From the solid green fabric, cut:
     11 strips, 2½" x 40" for borders.
     11 strips, 2¼" x 40" for binding
     2 strips, 14" x 40"; crosscut into 4 squares, 14" x 14" and 2 squares, 7¼" x 7¼"
     Cut each 14" square in half twice diagonally for side setting triangles.
     Cut each 7¼" square in half once for corner setting triangles.

Piecing the Yellow Leaf Blocks

The basic construction of this block is a nine-patch. The different elements that make up the nine-patch are half-square triangles, stem, signature square, and plain squares.

Half-Square Triangles

1. Draw a diagonal line on the back of the twenty-six 3⅞" background squares.

2. Pair a background square with a yellow print square. Stitch ¼" on either side of the drawn line.

3. Cut on the solid line and press. Make 52 half-square triangles.

Half-square triangles.

Stems

1. Sew a 4" background triangle to each side of a yellow-print 2" x 6½" rectangle.

2. Using a small square-up ruler, trim to 3½". Make 26. Be sure to lay the diagonal line of the ruler down the middle of the stem.

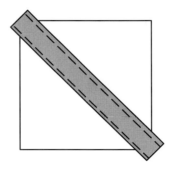

Signature Square

1. Mark a diagonal line on the back of the 2" yellow-print squares.

2. Place a print square on one corner of a 3½" background square.

3. Stitch on the marked line. Trim, leaving a ¼" seam allowance. Press. Make 26.

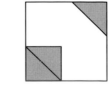

Signature square.

Assembling the Block

1. Lay out the blocks as shown, using the 3½" squares, half-square triangles, signature square, and stem square.

2. Join the squares into rows.

3. Join the rows together to form a block. Make 26.

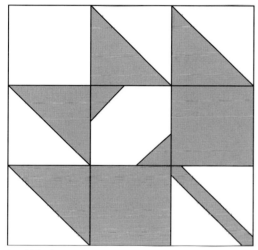

Leaf block.

Piecing the Green Leaf Blocks

1. Repeat the above steps to make 26 green leaf blocks.

Assembling the Top

1. Working on a design wall or on the floor, lay out the leaf blocks, setting squares, side setting triangles, and corner triangles. You will have one leaf block left over. This is perfect to use as a signature block on the back of your quilt.

2. Join the blocks together into diagonal rows.

3. Press the seams toward the setting blocks. This will allow the seams in each row to nest with the seams in the row below it.

4. Join the rows together. Press.

Adding the Borders
Inner and Filler Borders

1. Join the green strips for the inner border together by sewing diagonal seams. Join all of the strips together until you have one long strip. Press.

2. Join the yellow strips for the filler border together by sewing diagonal seams. Join all of the strips together until you have one long strip. Press.

3. Measure the width of your quilt through the middle. This will prevent you from having wavy borders. Mathematically, this number would be 64¼", but everyone's seam allowances vary, so be sure to measure.

4. Cut four green strips and two yellow strips the width of your quilt.

5. Sew a green strip to each side of a yellow strip. Repeat to make two.

 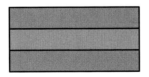

Filler borders.

6. Attach one to the top and one to the bottom of the quilt. Press.

7. Now measure your quilt lengthwise through the middle. This measurement should be approximately 78¼", but check your measurement to be sure.

8. Cut two green strips this length.

9. Add them to the sides of your quilt. Press.

Outer Borders

10. Repeat above steps, omitting the filler border.

Finishing Your Quilt

1. Cut your backing fabric into two equal pieces. Remove selvages and join together.

2. Prepare your quilt sandwich following the Layering and Basting instructions on page 121.

3. Avoid quilting in the signature squares of the quilt. The setting squares and triangles could lend themselves to some special designs.

4. Bind and label following the instructions for Straight of Grain, Double Fold Binding on page 122.

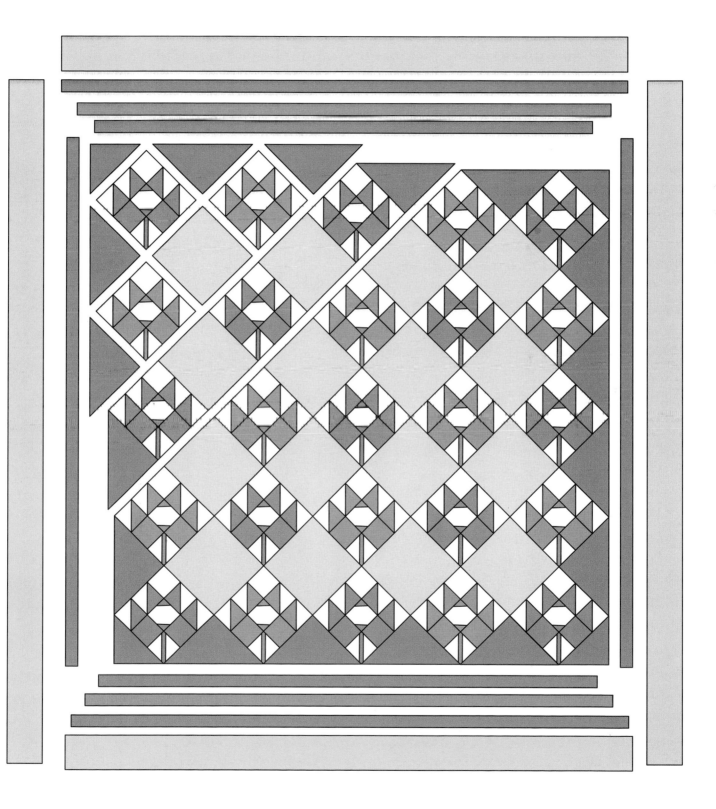

Reversible Picnic Cloth

These picnic cloths are so easy to make you might not be able to stop with just one. There are so many fun novelty prints available that are just beckoning to be used to brighten your next picnic. Don't limit yourself to picnics, though, these reversible cloths would look great on a table inside, too.

Fabric Requirements

Side A

1⅓ yd. main fabric

¾ yd. borders

Side B

1⅓ yd. main fabric

¾ yd. borders

Cutting Instructions

Side A

1. From main fabric, cut:
   - 1 strip, 6½" x 40"; crosscut into 4 squares, 6½" x 6½"
   - 1 square, 40½" x 40½"
2. From border fabric, cut:
   - 4 strips, 6½" x 40"

Side B

1. Repeat steps 1–2 above.

Piecing the Tablecloth

Side A

1. Sew a border strip to one side of the center square. Press toward border.

2. Sew a border strip to the opposite side of the center square. Press.

3. Add a 6½" square to both ends of remaining border strips. Press toward the border.

4. Sew strips to remaining sides of center square. Press.

Side B

5. Repeat steps 1–4 with Side B fabrics.

Tablecloth.

Finishing

1. Lay the two tablecloths right sides together.

2. Pin edges and sew with a ¼" seam, leaving a 5" opening for turning.

3. Turn right sides out. Press.

4. Blind stitch opening.

5. Top stitch edges, if desired.

Eva's Picnic Beans

My in-laws grew up in the shadow of Glacier National Park. At the drop of a hat the extended family would gather for a picnic on the shores of Lake McDonald. Everyone expected my mother-in-law to bring her popular Picnic Beans, and she never disappointed them! For a heartier version, brown and season a pound of ground beef and add to the mix.

Ingredients

15 ounce can chili with beans
15 ounce can green beans, drained
15 ounce can pork and beans
8 slices bacon, diced and browned
1 medium onion, diced
⅓ cup green pepper, diced
⅓ cup prepared chili sauce
⅓ cup brown sugar

Preparation

1. Mix all ingredients in a bean pot or casserole dish and bake uncovered for one hour at 350 degrees.

GENERAL INSTRUCTION

Rotary Cutting

Accurate cutting is the first step in making quilts that go together easily and lay flat. Proper tools make cutting easy. You will need a rotary cutter, an acrylic ruler, and a cutting mat.

When cutting, spread your fingers apart and place the fingertips on the half of the ruler that is closest to you. Do not lay your palm flat on the ruler. Place your rotary cutter next to the ruler and cut about half way across your fabric. Leaving your cutter in place, walk the fingers of the hand that is on the ruler up to the half of the ruler that is farthest from you. Press downward with your fingertips and continue making the cut.

Get familiar with your cutting tools and learn to read your ruler correctly. If you are cutting a lot of strips that are the same size, it can be helpful to put a narrow piece of masking tape on the back of the ruler at the proper measurement so you can quickly see that you are lining up properly.

Every brand of rotary cutter has a place on the top for your index finger. Wrap you fingers around the handle of the cutter, but be sure to place your index finger on the top. By placing your index finger on the top of your cutter, you have a straight line from your elbow. This is the ergonomically correct way to help you guide your cutter properly and won't lead to problems with your wrist or elbow.

Fabrics

Unless otherwise noted, the best fabrics for the quilts, wall hangings, and projects in this book are 100% cotton, quilt-weight fabrics. 100% cotton fabrics are easy to work with and press nicely, making it easy to match corners and points.

Threads

It's a good idea to match the fiber of the thread to the fiber of the fabric. In this case, that means using cotton thread for piecing and quilting.

You don't need many different colors of thread when piecing a quilt. A light gray and a dark gray work well for most patchwork.

Piecing/Seam Allowance

It is important to piece using a ¼" seam. Many sewing machines come with a ¼" foot, or a special ¼" foot can be purchased for them. If you do not have a ¼" foot, lay your acrylic ruler under your needle. Slowly, by hand, lower your needle until it just rests on the ¼" mark. Use a piece of masking tape on your machine bed to mark along the edge of ruler. This tape will act as a guide when sewing your seams.

Pressing

When quilting, seams are generally pressed to one side as opposed to being pressed open. When pressing seams to one side, it is very important to press from the front. Lay the pieced patches on the ironing board. Since you will usually want to press your seam toward the darker fabric, lay the pieced patch with the darker fabric on the top. This will automatically make the seam allowance lay toward the darker fabric when you separate the patches. Before opening, give the seam a quick press to help marry the sewing threads to the fabric. Then gently lift the top layer of fabric. Use the side of the iron to lay it over and press. By pressing from the front in this manner, you will avoid leaving little folds or pleats at the seams. These little pleats can have an adverse effect when you join your blocks or rows together.

Raw Edge Appliqué

With raw edge appliqué, the edge of the fabric isn't turned under. Cut the pieces to be appliquéd. Spray the wrong side of the appliqué pieces with a heat activated fusible spray, such as JT 606 spray. Once the spray has dried, it won't stick until heated with an iron. Place the appliqué pieces on the background fabric. Press with a hot, dry iron. Finish the edges by hand or machine.

To finish the edge by hand, use two strands of embroidery floss and a buttonhole stitch. To finish by machine, use a zigzag or satin stitch.

Borders

After piecing and assembling the quilt blocks, find a flat surface on which to lay the finished top. Using a tape measure, measure the length of the quilt through the middle. Cut two strips of border fabric this length. Find the center of the strip and the center of the quilt top. This can be done by folding the fabric in half and finger pressing. Pin the border strip to the quilt top at the center point. Next, pin the top and bottom edge. Continue pinning every few inches, easing if necessary. Sew the seam with a ¼" seam allowance. Press toward the border fabric.

Next, you will want to measure the width of the quilt top. Again, measure through the middle. This is what will assure that your finished top will lay flat. Cut two strips of border fabric this length. Find the centers, pin, stitch, and press. If there are multiple borders, repeat the above steps.

Backing

The backing of your quilt should be 4"–6" larger than the top. Excess will be trimmed away after quilting. When seaming backing pieces together, be sure to remove selvages. This will avoid puckering.

Batting

There are many choices of batting to use in your quilt. Batting can be made from natural fibers like cotton, wool, or even silk. It can also be made from polyester or a combination of a natural fiber and polyester. There are also different lofts, or thickness, to consider. Cotton blends work well for both hand and machine quilting. Cotton blends provide a flat look; are easy to care for; and are recommended for the projects in this book. Polyester batting usually has a higher loft. To avoid having the batting shift or lump up, check the label to see how close the quilting stitches need to be.

Layering and Basting

Once your quilt top is complete, you will need to make a quilt "sandwich" before you begin quilting. The quilt sandwich is made up of the quilt back, batting, and the pieced top. The backing and batting should be at least 4" larger than the quilt top.

1. After doing any necessary piecing of the backing fabric, tape the fabric, wrong side up, to a flat surface. Take care to insure that the fabric is pulled taut.

2. Lay the batting over the backing and smooth out any wrinkles.

3. Lay the well-pressed quilt top, right side up, on top of the batting.

4. If you will be hand quilting, baste with long running stitches. If you will be machine quilting, baste with safety pins.

Quilting

Quilting is the finishing touch in quilt making. All of the quilts and projects in this book give you suggestions for quilting designs, but feel free to experiment on your own.

If you aren't experienced quilting by hand or machine, there are many good books available on the subject.

Straight of Grain, Double Fold Binding

1. Cut binding strips 2¼" wide. Piece together with diagonal seams. Press seams open.

2. Press the binding in half lengthwise, wrong sides together.

3. Trim excess batting and backing from quilted top.

4. Beginning in the middle of one side of the quilt, place the folded binding strip right sides together along the edge of the quilt. The raw edges of the binding and the raw edges of the quilt should be together. Pin one side.

5. Beginning six or seven inches from the end of the binding strip, stitch with a ¼" seam. Stop stitching ¼" from the corner. Backstitch.

6. Pivot the quilt. Fold the binding strip up at a 45-degree angle then back down.

7. Begin sewing at the top edge of the quilt and continue around all four corners. Stop stitching approximately 3" from the beginning of the strip. This will leave 9"–10" of binding unsewn.

8. In the middle of this space, fold back the loose ends of the strips so they meet. Mark a dot along the fold at this point.

9. Open the binding strips. Pivot, aligning the dots, and sew the strips together with a diagonal seam.

10. Trim excess binding and stitch the unsewn area to quilt.

11. Fold the binding over the raw edge of the quilt so that it covers the machine stitching on the back side. Stitch in place using a blind stitch. A miter will form at the corners of your quilt.

Bias Binding

Note: *Bias binding is used when binding a curved edge. It is cut narrower and is a single fold, rather than a double fold, binding.*

1. Place fabric on cutting mat with selvages at either end.

2. Line the 45-degree mark on your ruler with the bottom edge of the fabric. Cut.

3. Cut 1½" strips.

4. Join the strips together at the short ends. Press seam open.

5. Follow steps 4–11 above, folding the raw edge under as you blind stitch the binding into place.

Labeling

Be sure to add a label to your quilt. Quilt labels can be simple or elaborate. A piece of muslin with the pertinent information written in permanent ink and whip stitched to the back of the quilt will suffice. If you are feeling more creative, you can embroider a label by hand or machine and embellish it with additional needlework. Photos transferred to fabric add a personal touch to a quilt. Decorative fabric labels are also available. These often have a floral design around the border and a blank area for you to add your personal information. Blind stitch the label to the back of your quilt.

Andover Fabrics, Inc.

1384 Broadway, Suite 1500
New York, NY 10018
(212) 710-1000
800-223-5678
www.andoverfabrics.com

Anna Lena's Quilt Shop

PO Box 1399
111 Bolstad Avenue
Long Beach, WA 98631
(360) 642-8585
www.annalena.com

Annie's Attic

1 Annie Lane
Big Sandy, TX 75755
(800) 582-6643
www.anniesattic.com

Keepsake Quilting

Route 25
P.O. Box 1618
Center Harbor, NH 03226-1618
(800) 438-5464
www.keepsakequilting.com

Krause Publications

(888) 457-2873
www.krause.com

Quilts from the Garden is Karen Snyder's third book. It follows the popular *Bundles of Fun* and *Fat Quarter Fun*. Besides designing quilts and authoring books, Karen owns Anna Lena's Quilt Shop and designs 1930s reproduction fabrics—called Wash Tub Prints—for Andover Fabrics.

Although she always knew that she would someday be a quilter, Karen didn't start quilting until 1995 when she received a free quilt pattern in the mail. Once she started hand piecing that Grandmother's Flower Garden, she was hooked and hasn't looked back.

Karen lives in Long Beach, Washington, with her husband, Bob Hamilton.

MIST KISSED

Lavender

Seed Packets Wall Hanging
Lavender
Increase 200%

No Better

Dill Weed

Seed Packets Wall Hanging
Dill Weed
Increase 200%

Seed Packets Wall Hanging
Parsley
Increase 200%

Parsley

BLUE RIBBON

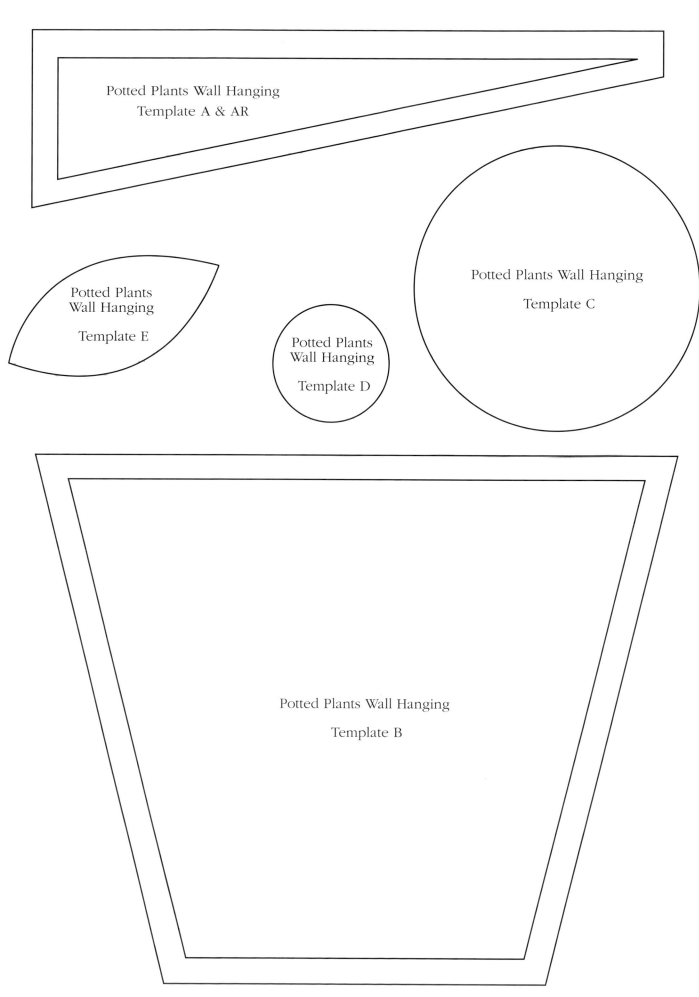

Potted Plants Wall Hanging
Template A & AR

Potted Plants
Wall Hanging

Template E

Potted Plants
Wall Hanging

Template D

Potted Plants Wall Hanging

Template C

Potted Plants Wall Hanging

Template B

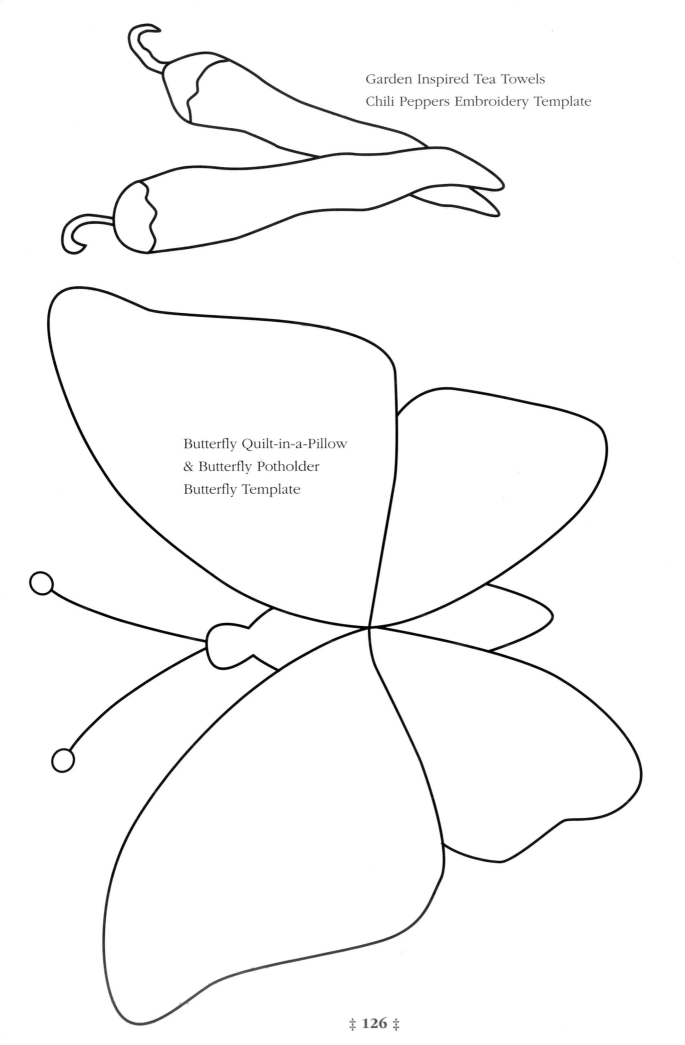

Garden Inspired Tea Towels
Chili Peppers Embroidery Template

Butterfly Quilt-in-a-Pillow
& Butterfly Potholder
Butterfly Template

Garden Inspired Tea Towels
Watermelon Slices Embroidery Template

Butterfly Quilt-in-a-Pillow
& Butterfly Potholder
Butterfly Template

ENHANCE YOUR QUILTING CREATIVITY AND EFFICIENCY

Quilts From Lavender Hill Farm

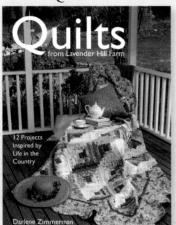

12 Projects Inspired by Life in the Country
by Darlene Zimmerman

The beauty and bounty at fictional Lavender Hill Farm is yours for the making, when you follow the detailed instructions – including 200+ breathtaking photos – of the 12 stunning quilt projects featured in this book.

Softcover • 8¼ x 10⅞ • 128 pages
25 color photos and 132 illustrations
Item# Z0380 • $22.99

Caliente Quilts

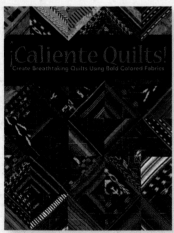

Create Breathtaking Quilts Using Bold Colored Fabrics
by Priscilla Bianchi

Learn to mix and match exotic fabrics from around the world for a fresh approach to contemporary quilts. Plus, you will enjoy learning from 120+ radiant photos of quilts and fabrics.

Softcover • 8¼ x 10⅞ • 144 pages
200+ color photos and illus.

Item# Z0103 • $24.99

Quilting Through the Seasons

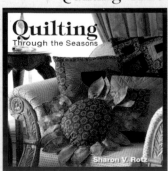

by Sharon Rotz

Fresh ideas, festive projects, and fantastic recipes await you, in this two-for-one book. Make a family celebration quilt, sunflower pillow, and related recipes including, salads with edible flowers.

Softcover • 8 x 8 • 160 pages
75 color photos
Item# Z0980 • $19.99

MORE FABRIC FUN FROM KAREN SNYDER

Bundles of Fun

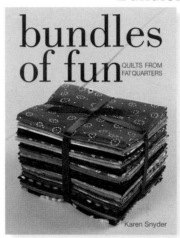

Quilts From Fat Quarters
by Karen Snyder

Discover fabric selection advice, instructions for making smaller quilts and adding sashing and borders within the details in this book. Plus, you'll explore variations for 12 coordinating projects.

Softcover • 8¼ x 10⅞ • 128 pages
150+ color photos and illus.
Item# FQLQ • $22.99

Fat Quarter Fun

by Karen Snyder

Indulge in the guilty pleasure of fat quarter quilts and you'll be glad you did, with 150 step-by-step photos, and 15+ projects, you'll find countless ways to have bundles of fun.

Softcover • 8¼ x 10⅞ • 128 pages
75 b&w illus. • 150 color photos

Item# Z0934 • $22.99

To order call 800-258-0929
• **Use coupon offer CRB8** •
or online at
www.krausebooks.com

krause publications
An imprint of F+W Publications, Inc.
700 East State Street • Iola WI 54990

Also available from select craft supply shops and booksellers nationwide.